Why *do we* BELIEVE?

Why *do we* BELIEVE?

Fr. Benedict J. Groeschel, CFR

Our Sunday Visitor Publishing Division
Our Sunday Visitor, Inc.
Huntington, IN 46750

Copyright © 2005 by Our Sunday Visitor Publishing Division
Our Sunday Visitor, Inc.   Published 2005

10 09 08 07 06 05   1 2 3 4 5 6 7 8 9

Our Sunday Visitor Publishing Division
Our Sunday Visitor, Inc.
200 Noll Plaza
Huntington, IN 46750

ISBN: 1-59276-049-X (Inventory No. T100)
LCCN: 2005931301

Cover design by Alex Kubik
Cover Image by Fr. John Lynch
Interior design by Sherri L. Hoffman

PRINTED IN THE UNITED STATES OF AMERICA

This little book is dedicated to
His Holiness Pope Benedict XVI,
a faithful and true Christian.

Let not your hearts be troubled;
believe in God, believe also in me.

JN 14:1

Contents

Acknowledgments

I am very grateful to Michael Dubruiel of Our Sunday Visitor for encouraging me to do this small but convenient book for people who are having trouble with faith or who are trying to increase their faith. It is purposely short and to the point. In order to make the book available quickly, I have relied on the help of my editor, Charles Pendergast. I am also grateful to Alex Kubik and Fr. John Lynch for the cover art and design and for their encouragement in completing the manuscript.

Without prayer, growth in faith could not take place. I hope that every reader will approach this work in a prayerful way and will include a prayer for me.

FR. BENEDICT J. GROESCHEL, C.F.R.

April 21, 2005

Feast of St. Conrad of Bavaria, O.F.M. Cap.

Introduction

The Catholic Church in the United States is currently going through one of the great crises of its history — a crisis of faith. The faith of many good and even devout people is shaken. Even when we are not in times of crisis, our faith is constantly challenged — by secularism, skepticism, unbelief, a lack of faith, and the temptations of the world.

In this little book I wish to address the need for a renewal of faith, concentrating on three areas of belief: faith in God, faith in Christ, and faith in the Church of Christ. I address this presentation to believers and unbelievers alike. I hope it will strengthen the former and give to those who do not believe at least some understanding of what motivates such a large number of their fellow human beings.

I.

Faith in God

"Jesus answered them, 'Have faith in God.'"
Mk 11:22

Many years ago, just after World War II, the great Dominican friar and theologian Fr. Reginald Garrigou-Lagrange was scheduled to lecture on "De Deo Uno" (On the One God) at the Pontifical University of Saint Thomas Aquinas in Rome, often known as the *Angelicum*. He came into the lecture hall, which was jammed. Everyone wanted to hear Father Garrigou-Lagrange. He said a prayer and then began his lecture.

"God . . ." Then he hesitated. He repeated, "God . . ." Finally he cleared his throat and in a quiet voice began again a third time. "God . . ." And then silence. Father Garrigou-Lagrange could not speak. He folded his papers and left the podium. He was so overcome by the thought of what this word meant that he could say no more. Those present never forgot this amazing event, which was far more memorable than a lecture.

In the epistle to the Hebrews we read these words, based on Psalm 102, which perhaps catch some of the thoughts in the great theologian's mind that day:

> Thou, Lord, didst found the earth in the beginning, and the heavens are the work of thy hands; they will perish, but thou remainest; they will all grow old like a garment, like a mantle thou wilt roll them up, and they will be changed. But thou art the same, and thy years will never end (Heb 1:10-12).

Ninety-four percent of the people in the United States say they believe in a personal God who knows them. Of the same group, 92 percent say they believe in a God they will meet at the end of their lives and to whom they will have to render an account of all that they have done or not done during their time on earth. (Although very large, the number of believers is hardly recognized by the secular media in the United States, which constantly mocks and belittles religion. This reveals how far removed the media moguls are from any real understanding of the

American people.) Ninety-four percent believe that there is a God who knows they exist and who personally cares about their existence!

Now this is immensely mysterious. How can anyone — even a divine being — know the six and a half billion people who live on the earth?

In relation to this mystery our Divine Savior, Jesus Christ, says:

> Are not two sparrows sold for a penny? And not one of them will fall to the ground without your Father's will. But even the hairs of your head are all numbered. Fear not, therefore; you are of more value than many sparrows (Mt 10:29-31).

GOD KNOWS EVERYTHING

If you look into distant space, you can see the star Epsilon Aurigae, which is 2,000 light-years away. If you've got really good eyes and know where to look, you can see the great Andromeda Nebula, which is two million light-years away. In order to calculate the distance, you would have to multiply two million by almost six trillion miles (the distance light travels in one year). And cosmically speaking, the Andromeda Nebula is our next-door neighbor! If you find that distance staggering, keep in mind that there are billions of galaxies of billions of stars in the universe, most of which are at unimaginable distances from Earth. And God knows them all and has given each a name.

> He determines the number of the stars,
> he gives to all of them their names
> (Ps 147:4).

In New York we rarely have a good view of the stars and their constellations. Atmospheric conditions and the millions of man-made lights militate against this. But occasionally, on a numbingly cold night in January or a crisp evening in early fall, even we New Yorkers are favored with a display of God's majesty revealed in the heavens.

If you live in a rural area, especially near a desert, the next time you look into the night sky and contemplate the beauty of God's creation, thank Him and be humbled. Realize your rather insignificant place in what to the human mind seems a limitless universe and which is, in fact, a glimpse of the secret of God's infinity. Remember your position before God, who, allegorically speaking, could hold dozens of universes in the palm of His hand. We, on the other hand, are made of the dust of the earth, and our lives come and go in the blink of an eye. We must all learn the lesson taught to Job long ago when God questioned him:

"Is it at thy command the glittering bright Pleiades cluster so close, and Orion's circlet spreads so wide? Dost thou tell the day star when to shine out, the evening star when to rise over the sons of earth?" (Job 38:31–32).[1]

God is God, and we are not. If we try arrogantly to usurp His place, the result is both pathetic and destructive. Man's only logical response to God is faith and awe.

The number of stars that God has created is so great that if you reduced every star — not every planet, but every star — to a grain of sand, do you know how large a container you would need to hold the grains of sand? You can fit 2.5 million grains into an eight-ounce glass. If we had a box that could hold all the grains of sand, each one of them representing a star, the box to hold them would be a mile high and a mile across, and it would extend from New York City to a point beyond Key West, Florida.

SHOULDN'T EVERYONE BE INTERESTED IN GOD?

Some people tell me very nonchalantly, "Oh yes, I believe in God." Quite frankly, I'd rather talk to atheists, because at least they will argue with you about God and take seriously the concept of

God. Some atheists care more about the question of God than many of those who mouth belief in God. Some who call themselves believers parrot statements like, "Well, I think there is a God — you know, the Man Upstairs." There's hope for the conversion of an atheist. He is looking for something. He has no meaning, no place to go — no up, no down, no beginning, no end. Some people will tell you: "Well, I believe in God, but I don't go to church. I don't even pray very often, because God knows what I'm thinking. He knows what I need." Those people are "schlepping it," as we say in New York. Someone who talks like that about God is schlepping his or her way through life — toward a big surprise.

GOD IS MYSTERY

Let's begin with the most important idea, which receives little recognition in contemporary culture: God is mystery. God is not just mysterious. He is mystery itself.

Mystery comes from the Greek word *mystein*, meaning "to close your eyes." God is invisible and utterly mysterious. Personally, I happen to love mystery. If something does not have a mystery about it, I'm not even slightly interested, because it represents the narrowness of the human mind.

For those impressed by science, do you know that science is filled with mysteries? If I drop anything from my hand, it will fall to the floor. Why? Gravity. A good scientist can tell you how fast the object will fall depending on its size and proximity to the earth, but nobody has the slightest idea what gravity is. Are there invisible chains that cause the object to go down rather than up? It's a mystery!

Who knows what life is? The philosophical biologists tell us that if something doesn't wiggle around and leave messes after itself, it's a rock. That's one definition of life in scientific terms — a bit simplified, I admit.

What is time? St. Augustine says, "If you don't ask me what time is, I know, but if you ask me, I can't tell you." Time is also a mystery.

Let's say we have an astronaut — let's make her a woman astronaut. She is going to travel at slightly less than the speed of light to the nearest star, which is four and a half light-years away, reaching her destination in almost five years. She will take a couple of trips around the star and then return, arriving back on Earth in about ten years. She will have traveled at a little less than 186,000 miles a second, logging about 5.8 trillion miles a year — give or take a few feet.

When our astronaut splashes down in the Pacific, many ships and all the media will greet her. She will get out of her space capsule and board one of the ships. On deck she will meet several very elderly people. They will be her great-great-great grandchildren. During her travels at slightly less than the speed of light for ten years, two hundred years would have elapsed on Earth. That's an application of the FitzGerald-Lorentz observation of the contraction of time at very high speeds. I didn't make it up. This is science. It is a natural mystery, and this is why one of my favorite proponents of mystery is the greatest scientist who ever lived, Albert Einstein.

Einstein said:

> The fairest thing we can experience is the mysterious. It is the fundamental emotion which stands at the cradle of true art and science. . . . A knowledge of the existence of something we cannot penetrate, of the manifestations of the profoundest reason and the most radiant beauty, which are only accessible to our reason in their most elementary forms — it is this knowledge and this emotion that constitute the truly religious attitude.[2]

We live in a world of people who think they have everything all figured out. Every day I pray for the conversion of those who write most of the high school science textbooks. The League of the Militant Godless generally could not be more hostile to faith than these people are. In fact, it must unfortunately be said that these textbook authors show a certain density or stupidity. They need all the prayers they can get.

What did Albert Einstein say about all this? He held that there were two kinds of people: those who thought nothing was a miracle and those who thought everything was a miracle. He identified himself with the second group.

Einstein met some priests I know, and all he ever wanted to talk to them about was the Blessed Sacrament of the Catholic Church — yes, the Holy Eucharist, especially the idea of a substance that has no accidents, no appearances, no length, width, size, color, or shape. It was one of Einstein's favorite mysteries. Fr. Charles McTeague, who is still living today in Newark, New Jersey, recalls discussing this divine mystery with Einstein and the great man's request for German theology books on the subject.

God is mysterious, and His Church — the Catholic Church — is a church of mystery.

I get annoyed sometimes, particularly with some Catholic intellectuals, because they think they have everything explained. What they cannot explain they ignore, which is perhaps the stupidest thing anyone can do. Their technique is to pretend not to notice what cannot be explained. Don't look at the elephant sitting in the living room.

Some people claim that if they say their prayers, they need not go to church, from which they derive little anyway. Others maintain: "I don't really care what the Church says. I just go in order to have my passport stamped so that the day I die I get into heaven."

One of the great theologians of the nineteenth century, Fr. Matthias Scheeben, says:

> Christianity entered the world as a religion replete with mysteries. It was proclaimed as the mystery of Christ in Romans and Colossians and as a mystery of the Kingdom of God by Christ Himself in Mark and Luke. Its ideas and doctrines were unknown, unprecedented, and they were to remain forever inscrutable and unfathomable.[3]

Inscrutable means you can't investigate or search something, and unfathomable means you can't get to the bottom. This is why I become angry when somebody says something so stupid as, "Christ didn't know who He was." Christ is the most mysterious Person who ever lived! Our blessed Mother in eternal glory does not understand everything about the thinking of her Son, but there are a few people around today who will say, "Oh, I don't think Jesus knew who He was." Please! Don't insult our intelligence.

Father Scheeben says, "The greater, the more sublime, and the more divine Christianity is, the more inexhaustible, inscrutable, unfathomable, and mysterious its subject matter must be." He goes on to point out that Jesus would give a very poor account of Himself as the Son of God if He revealed to us only things that we could have deduced by our own minds. Likewise, the Holy Spirit — the Spirit of Truth — would be a very sorry God indeed if He revealed only things that we already knew by our own mind.

John Henry Cardinal Newman was one of the great converts of the nineteenth century. In order to point out to the Catholics of his time, especially the sophisticated Catholics, that they did not have to apologize for the Church, he wrote the following in his *Idea of a University*:

Catholicism, as it has come down to us from the first, seems to be mean and illiberal; it is a mere popular religion; it is the religion of illiterate ages or servile populations or barbarous warriors; it must be treated with discrimination and delicacy, corrected, softened, improved, if it is to satisfy an enlightened generation. It must be stereotyped as the patron of arts, or the pupil of speculation, or the protégé of science; it must play the literary academician, or the empirical philanthropist, or the political partisan; it must keep up with the age; some or other expedient it must devise in order to explain away, or to hide, tenets under which the intellect labors and of which it is ashamed — its doctrine, for instance, of grace, its mystery of the Godhead, its preaching of the Cross, its devotion to the Queen of Saints, or its loyalty to the Apostolic See.

Let this spirit be freely evolved out of ... [a] philosophical condition of mind ... and it is impossible but, first indifference, then laxity of belief, then even heresy will be the successive results.[4]

Yet there are those around right now who think they are going to buttress the faith, strengthen the Church, and make it agreeable to the world by taking away its mystery. In effect, they are simply chipping away at the Church's foundations and taking the most beautiful jewel from its crown.

FAITH: THE WAY TO APPROACH MYSTERY

In order to approach mystery, you have to have faith. Faith, unfortunately, can mean different things, and religious faith itself comes in degrees. To the Samaritan leper who returned to thank Our Lord for his cure, Jesus said: "Your faith has saved you." And He reproached His own disciples for their lack of faith and for having little faith.

Someone might ask, "Do you have any religion?"

And another might respond, "Yes. I believe in the Catholic religion."

"Do you go to church?"

"No," the other may answer surprisingly. And then, clarifying: "Well, after automobile accidents I go to church. I'll go to church next Sunday just for you."

One man said to me, "My mother is a religious fanatic."

"Why? What does she do?" I asked.

"She goes to Mass every Sunday."

We are supposed to go to Mass every Sunday! It's one of the Ten Commandments: "Remember to keep holy the Lord's day."

What does it really mean to believe, to have faith?

Newman said:

A religious mind is ever marveling, and irreligious men laugh and scoff at it because it marvels. A religious mind is ever looking out of itself, is ever pondering God's words, is ever "looking into" them with the Angels, is ever realizing to itself Him on whom it depends, and who is the centre of all truth and good. Carnal and proud minds are content with self; they like to remain at home; when they hear of mysteries, they have no devout curiosity to go and see the great sight, though it be ever so little out of their way; and when it actually falls in their path, they stumble at it. As great then as is the difference between hanging upon the thought of God and resting in ourselves, lifting up the heart to God and bringing all things in heaven and earth down to ourselves, exalting God and exalting reason, measuring things by God's power and measuring them by our own ignorance, so great is the difference between him who believes in the Christian mysteries and him who does not. And were there no other reason for the revelation of them but this gracious one, of raising us, refining us, making us reverent, making us expectant and devout, surely this would be more than a sufficient one.[5]

One day, as I was walking past a nursing home in Greenwich Village, I came on a very old man sitting there, getting the sun. I walked up to him and said hello. I realized that he was almost blind.

"Hello," he answered.

"My name is Father Benedict."

He suddenly gave me his name and said, "You know, Father, I'm a Catholic. I'm going to heaven. I believe in Jesus Christ. I believe He saved me, and I'm sorry for my sins. I'm going to heaven." This little poor old man knows more than most of the people who live in New York City.

A friend of mine, Ruby Davis, is a little old African-American woman who comes to us for the baskets that our community distributes in the South Bronx each Thanksgiving, Christmas, and Easter. She is always smiling.

Once I said to her, "Ruby, why are you always smiling?"

"Oh," she said, "because I'm so grateful to God."

"What for?" I asked her.

Ruby replied, "I can see. I can hear. I can talk, and I can walk. And when I get finished here, I'm going straight up to heaven like a shootin' star." Ruby is very wise. I have been a psychologist for thirty-five years, and I don't know too many of my fellow psychologists who have their act together as well as Ruby Davis.

WHAT IS FAITH?

In answering that question, Newman advises us to look beyond this world to God. Faith moves us to try to learn as much about God as we can and to seek the blessings we need from Him.

> What is meant by faith? It is to feel in good earnest that we are creatures of God; it is a practical perception of the unseen world; it is to understand that this world is not enough for our happiness, to look beyond it on towards God, to realize His presence, to wait upon Him, to endeavor to learn and to do His will, and to seek our good from Him. It is not a mere temporary strong act or impetuous feeling of the mind, an impression or a view coming upon it, but it is a habit, a state of mind, lasting and consistent. To have faith in God is to surrender oneself to God, humbly to put one's interests, or to wish to be allowed to put them, into His hands who is the Sovereign Giver of all good.[6]

Faith should possess you. If it doesn't — to use the words of Jesus — "You have little faith." He said that to the people of His time. "O men of little faith" (Mt 8:26; Lk 12:28). And to the Canaanite woman who believed that He could work a miracle to save her daughter Jesus said, "Woman, great is your faith!" (Mt 15:28).

FAITH REQUIRES OBEDIENCE TO GOD

We know, therefore, from Christ Himself that there is great faith and little faith. An essential part of faith, as Newman reminds us, is obedience, a virtue largely forgotten in our time.

Now, again, let me ask, what is obedience? It is the obvious mode, suggested by nature, of a creature's conducting himself in God's sight, who fears Him as his Maker, and knows that as a sinner, he has especial cause for fearing Him. Under such circumstances he "will do what he can" to please Him, as the woman whom our Lord commended. He will look every way to see how it is possible to approve himself to Him, and will rejoice to find any service which may stand as a sort of proof that he is in earnest. And he will find nothing better as an offering, or as an evidence, than obedience to that

Holy Law, which conscience tells him has been given us by God Himself; that is, he will be diligent in doing all his duty as far as he knows it and can do it. Thus, as is evident, the two states of mind are altogether one and the same: it is quite indifferent whether we say a man seeks God in faith, or say he seeks Him by obedience. . . .[7]

If you have great faith, you do not want to avoid obeying the divine law; rather, you want to find the best way to observe the divine law. You want to go first class, which means doing something as well as possible.

Do you know what a saint is? A saint is someone who always goes forward with faith.

But in very truth, from the beginning to the end of Scripture, the one voice of inspiration consistently maintains, not a uniform contrast between faith and obedience, but this *one* doctrine, that the only way of salvation open to us is the surrender of ourselves to our Maker in all things — supreme devotion, resignation of our will, the turning with all our heart to God.[8]

WE NEED FAITH, HOPE, AND LOVE

Our Divine Savior says, "Seek first his kingdom and his righteousness, and all these things shall be yours as well" (Mt 6:33). We need to have faith. Faith is immensely important, and it is a tragedy that it is so weak in our time.

St. Paul tells us: "Therefore, since we are justified by faith, we have peace with God through our Lord Jesus Christ. Through him we have obtained access to this grace in which we stand, and we rejoice in our hope of sharing the glory of God" (Rom 5:1-2). Faith is the entrance to the way of salvation. Many people get involved in that useless old argument over faith and works. I never met good Protestants who didn't think they should obey God's will, and I never met good Catholics who thought they would get to heaven just by doing good works, such as giving away turkeys at Thanksgiving. According to St. Paul, we are saved not only by faith but also by hope. "For in this hope we were saved. Now hope that is seen is not hope. For who hopes for what he sees? But if we hope for what we do not see, then we wait for it with patience" (Rom 8:24).

But faith and hope are not all. We need charity, too. Our Divine Savior Himself teaches this forcefully.

When the Son of Man comes in his glory, and all the angels with him, then he will sit on his glorious throne. Before him will be gathered all the nations, and he will separate them one from another as a shepherd separates the sheep from the goats, and he will place the sheep at his right hand, but the goats at the left. Then the King will say to those at his right hand, "Come, O blessed of my Father, inherit the kingdom prepared for you from the foundation of the world; for I was hungry and you gave me food, I was thirsty and you gave me drink, I was a stranger and you welcomed me" (Mt 25:31-35).

Faith, hope, and charity are the road to the kingdom of God, the road to salvation. Of course, none of these really saves us. Our Savior is Our Lord Jesus Christ, and He alone. We must believe in Him as we believe in God, the Creator of the universe, because Christ is the Son of God. Faith, hope, and love are the way to salvation and eternal life. But the Savior — the author of all saving grace — is Jesus, the Son of God.

II.

Faith in Christ

Jesus said to him, "Have you believed because you have seen me? Blessed are those who have not seen and yet believe."
JN 20:29

FALSE CHRISTS

In the first chapter, I wrote about why we need a deep faith in God, a subject that could fill hundreds of volumes. In this chapter we will ask the question, "Why should we believe in Jesus Christ?"

It should be clearly understood that I refer to the Christ of faith. I am not talking about the false Christ of the New Age, an image that has much in common with countless gurus and avatars. Nor am I thinking of the false Christ who was the nicest man who ever lived and consequently God adopted Him as His son. I do not even speak of the false Christ who is a lesser god. That would be Arianism, a heresy condemned by the Church in A.D. 325, but unfortunately still very much with us. When I speak of faith, I mean the One of whom St. John says:

> For God so loved the world that he gave his only Son, that whoever believes in Him should not perish but have eternal life. For God sent the Son into the world, not to condemn the world, but that the world might be saved through him (Jn 3:16-17).

Some years ago there was a popular movie called "Oh, God!" in which one of my favorite old comic actors, George Burns, played God. At one point someone asks "God": "Is Jesus Christ your son?" This God paused and said, "Of course Jesus is my son, but then everybody is my son and my daughter." It was a subtle attack on our faith, done in a quaint and seemingly innocent fashion, reducing Christ to just another human being, like you and me.

Every year newsmagazines run stories about Jesus, usually at Christmas and Easter. Who is quoted in these stories? A very select group of scholars — and I use the term reluctantly — who call themselves the Jesus Seminar. They also get air time from public television. Their argument is an old one. They try to make you think that Jesus Christ was not really the Son of God.

Where can we learn about Jesus Christ and who He is? We discover Him in the New Testament.

Where do we get the New Testament? Evangelists and other men chosen by God wrote the books of the New Testament under the inspiration of the Holy Spirit, and the early Church recognized their writings as being inspired. The last two books of the Bible were approved in A.D. 398 by the bishops of the Catholic Church, the only people who had authority to approve them. These books were the epistle to the Hebrews and the book of Revelation, which were approved by the Catholic bishops of Africa. And, finally, Pope Damasus approved the whole list of books, or canon, in 401.

Now, this is where our knowledge of Jesus Christ comes from, and I want to emphasize that there is, among many people, an immense amount of skepticism concerning the books of the New Testament — in fact, about the whole Bible. The word of God, that is, the Bible, is frequently treated like the words of men. If you are at a college, or someone you know is, where they offer a course called "The Bible as Literature," don't take it! Take cooking instead. Take atomic physics. Take calculus. Take anything — even golf — but don't take "The Bible as Literature."

The course will probably be taught by someone who never read the Bible and accepted it as the word of God. Moreover, it will take away the mystery and the supernatural element of Sacred Scripture and destroy any appreciation of the Bible as the word of God.

THE REAL JESUS[9]

Let's take a serious look at Our Lord and Savior Jesus Christ. He lived in Nazareth, a little hamlet of some two hundred souls; today it is a fairly large town. He wasn't born there; He was born in Bethlehem and laid in a manger because there was no room for the Holy Family in the inn. You know the account.

When Christ was a young man, perhaps twenty-nine or thirty, it came to be His turn to read in the synagogue what is called the *haftorah*. The first readings in the synagogue service are taken from the Torah, made up of the first five books of the Bible. Next come the *haftorah*, verses from the Prophets. The Gospels tell us that when Our Lord read the *haftorah*, He opened the scroll and found the place where it was written in the book of Isaiah: "The spirit of the Lord is upon me, because he has anointed me to preach good news to the poor. He has sent me to proclaim release to the captives and recovering of sight to the blind, to set at liberty those who are oppressed, to proclaim the acceptable year of the Lord" (Lk 4:18-19). He returned the scroll to the attendant, "and the eyes of all in the synagogue were fixed on him" as He said, "Today this scripture has been fulfilled in your hearing" (Lk 4:20-21).

Many of the people who heard Our Lord read this passage were His kinsmen, some of whom were not very kind. Eventually they would try to throw Him off a cliff. Some of them thought they were His relatives, but they did not know of His miraculous conception by the power of the Holy Spirit at the word of the archangel to Mary. How do we know this? Because the only possible witness could be the person who gave those words to St. Luke, or the source he relied on, and that was Mary herself.

Some people would say cynically, "Well, you know, I mean, really." It's a little too much for them. Consider, however, that God brought into existence the entire universe and that some scientists estimate the number of known stars at 70 sextillion — that is, 7 followed by 22 zeros. Obviously, then, God could, since He has made all life, cause that little infant to begin to exist in the womb of His Mother in whatever way He chose.

The world has trouble with Jesus Christ because He is mysterious and divine. One of our Presidents, Thomas Jefferson, wrote an extraordinarily stupid book. It was a life of Christ, but without miracles. Jefferson himself had an almost miraculous ability to say stupid things about Christ. It was really almost inspired, but not by God.

Take the four Gospels and with a razor blade cut out all the references to Christ's divinity, to His oneness with the Father and His divine power (there are 230 of them). What have you got left? Confetti! And that is what some teachers do.

Playing down Christ's divinity is a phenomenon that occurs, I am sorry to say, even in some schools that call themselves Christian or Catholic. Jesus Christ? What is He? Who is He? We have it stated so beautifully in the Gospel of St. John: "For God so loved the world that he gave his only Son, that whoever believes in him should not perish but have eternal life. For God sent the Son into the world, not to condemn the world, but that the world might be saved through him" (Jn 3:16-17). Everyone should memorize this passage.

What does it mean to assert that Jesus Christ is our Savior? I go back to Newman, the great scholar and teacher. He says, "Christ, we are told, has gone up on high" — and he's quoting Scripture — "'to present Himself before the face of God for us.' He has 'entered by His own blood once for all into the Holy Place, having affected eternal redemption.' 'He ever liveth to make intercession for those who come unto God by Him; He hath a priesthood which will not pass from Him.' 'We have such an High Priest, who is set on the right hand of the throne of the Majesty in the heavens; a Minister of the Sanctuary, and of the true Tabernacle, which the Lord pitched, and not man.'" (See Heb 9, 7, and 8.)[10]

THE TROUBLE WITH CHRIST

The world has trouble with Christ, and I'm sorry to say that it is probably because of pride. Did you ever wonder whether you would really like to meet someone who was divine? Everybody would say, "Oh, I'd love to see Jesus." Are you sure? I have worked with a couple of very holy people who were very close to Christ, one being Mother Teresa. It wasn't a lot of fun. I knew Mother Teresa half my life — 32 out of my 64 years — when she died. I believe with very good reason that she operated on inspiration, and there was no use arguing with her. Believe me, I tried. I had many arguments with Mother Teresa, and I lost them all in an attempt to fit her into the Church's ongoing apostolate. This apostolate is governed by committees, decisions, and information. That is not what Mother Teresa operated on.

But ultimately who and what was Mother Teresa? She was just another one of us poor sinners, but she had powerfully surrendered to God and seemed to know His will often enough. What would it be like if you met a man who *is* God?

What about the apostles? When one of them tried to argue with Our Lord, He said, "Get behind me, Satan" (Mt 16:23). How would you like to meet somebody who knows all about you? Someone who knows more about you than you know about yourself? Someone who can see into the depths of your soul and who knows what will happen to you after death? Somebody who can tell you to do something and you cannot argue? It could be very intimidating.

We all have our own idea of what God should do. So did the apostles. Our Lord had promised them that they would judge the twelve tribes of Israel (see Mt 19: 28). They expected Him to set up an earthly kingdom. He worked miracles in the boondocks, up in the woods, healing lepers and blind people. The apostles had their own ideas of what He should do. Perhaps they thought he should go to Jerusalem and turn the gates of the temple to gold. Or turn the arms and spears of the Roman soldiers to butter? No. God will be God, and He will not ask us what we think He should do.

There are no examples in Scripture of Jesus asking for anyone's advice. The only person who *appears* to have won a bit of an argument with Him is His mother. He apparently did not want to work a miracle at the wedding feast at Cana when the family ran out of wine, but His mother prevailed. He was a good Jewish boy who listened to His mother. In a way He still does.

WHO IS CHRIST?

Who is Christ? According to early Church teaching, Jesus Christ is a divine Person, "God from God, light from light, true God from true God, begotten not made, one in being with the Father." He is of one substance with the Father (in Greek, *homoousios*, of one substance). Jesus Christ is not a human person. He has a human nature and a divine nature, but He is only and simply a divine Person.

This is the doctrine of the Catholic Church and of the Eastern Orthodox churches. Both mutually accept the doctrines of the first seven ecumenical councils, beginning with the Council of Nicea in the year 325 and ending with the Third Council of Constantinople in 681. Moreover, none of the reformers at the time of the Protestant Reformation disagreed with the teaching of Christ's divinity. Neither Luther nor Calvin ever disagreed with the early conciliar teachings. If you are an evangelical or other type of Protestant, you also should agree with them, even though you may not know about them, in order to be loyal to your own heritage.

A fifth-century archbishop of Constantinople, Nestor, said that Mary was the mother of the human Jesus and that God was the father of the divine Word. He was condemned at the Council of Ephesus (A.D. 431), which proclaimed Mary as *Theotokos*, a Greek word that means God-bearer or Mother of God, that is, the mother of a person who is divine. Protestants do not like this title for the Blessed Virgin Mary. But if you ask a well-instructed Protestant minister, he will probably tell you, "We don't like the title, but we better not say anything else, or we will end up with two people, Jesus of Nazareth and the Son of God."

Were there two people? No! There was only one Person. What did this divine Person, Jesus Christ, do? He saved us.

How did He do it? St. Paul tells us in his Letter to the Philippians:

> Have this mind among yourselves, which was in Christ Jesus, who, though he was in the form of God, did not count equality with God a thing to be grasped, but emptied himself, taking the form of a servant, being born in the likeness of men. And being found in human form he humbled himself and became obedient unto death, even death on a cross (Phil 2:5-8).

That is what Our Lord did, and what happened?

> Therefore God has highly exalted him and bestowed on him the name which is above every name, that at the name of Jesus every knee should bow, in heaven and on earth and under the earth, and every tongue confess that Jesus Christ is Lord, to the glory of God the Father (Phil 2:9-11).

What does the word *Lord* mean? In the Old Testament — the Jewish Scriptures — as well as in the New, it means God.

Some people tell me they don't need the Church, but where will they learn all these things? They might say, "Well, I'll get it out of the Bible." But where did the Bible come from? The Old Testament came from the Jews. From the authority of the teachers of the Jewish tradition they determined that these books were part of God's revelation; they were the word of God. They became the Scriptures.

But in the New Testament, who has the authority? Only one group of people. In ancient Greek they were called *episcopoi*, the overseers. In English we translate this as bishop. No matter what Christian denomination you belong to, every time you pick up a New Testament, you have accepted the authority of the bishops of the ancient Catholic Church.

Where does the word *Catholic* come from? Once, when I was in Greece with a group of priests on pilgrimage, I was trying, with my modest knowledge of New Testament Greek, to read the Greek signs. During our travels we passed a big service station, which sold gasoline, and I also noticed a sign that read WE FIX CATHOLICS.

I said to the priests traveling with me, "I'll go right in. This is great. Let's see what they can do." The Greek word *catoholoi* (like the English word *catholic*) means universal. In this case the service station was advertising the fact that they could fix universal joints, a part found on a truck.

EXPERIENCING OUR LORD

Most people believe in Christ because they have had some experience of Him. Perhaps they have been desperate or mired in sin. They may have gone through a period of hopelessness, when their lives had no meaning. In desperation they cried out to God and somehow knew that Christ was there. If that has never happened to you, pray and be attentive. It will.

Archbishop Anthony Bloom, the Russian Orthodox archbishop of England, was, in early life, an atheist. As a refugee from the Bolshevik revolution, he lived in Paris, where he was a student. Many years later he wrote a book in which he describes a conversion experience.

> One day — it was during Lent, and I was then a member of one of the Russian youth organizations in Paris — one of the leaders came up to me and said, "We have invited a priest to talk to you. Come." I answered with violent indignation that I would not. I had no use for the Church. I did not believe in God. I didn't want to waste any of my time. . . .
>
> I sat through the lecture. I didn't intend to listen. But my ears pricked up. I became more and more indignant. I saw a vision of

Christ and Christianity that was profoundly repulsive to me. When the lecture was over, I hurried home in order to check the truth of what he had been saying. I asked my mother whether she had a book of the Gospel, because I wanted to know whether the Gospel would support the monstrous impression I had derived from his talk. I expected nothing good from my reading, so I counted the chapters of the four Gospels to be sure I read the shortest, not to waste time unnecessarily. I started to read St. Mark's Gospel.

While I was reading the beginning of St. Mark's Gospel, before I reached the third chapter, I suddenly became aware that on the other side of my desk there was a presence. And the certainty was so strong that it was Christ standing there that it has never left me. This was the real turning point. Because Christ was alive and I had been in his presence I could say with certainty that what the Gospel said about the crucifixion of the Prophet of Galilee was true, and the centurion was right when he said, "Truly he is the Son of God." It was in the light of the Resurrection that I could read with certainty the story of the Gospel, knowing that everything was true in it because the impossible event of the Resurrection was to me more certain than any event of history.[11]

If you are not a believer, I cannot communicate belief to you. I cannot communicate Archbishop Bloom's belief or mine, but I can tell you that I have believed very truly in Christ since I was seven years old. I remember the day, the hour, the minute, and the place. And my belief has continued to grow.

Sometimes I wonder what I would be without Christ. The thought is frightening. Oh, I wouldn't be a criminal. I hope I would not be an alcoholic or a drug addict or a fugitive from the police. But I would probably be half of what I am right now. I'd be a psychologist, or perhaps a psychiatrist, and I'd live in some wealthy suburb and charge $150 an hour to lead people from a state of misery to one of mere unhappiness. I would probably have a couple of yuppie kids bellyaching because I didn't give them more money, and I would certainly be married at least twice because nobody in their right mind could put up with me. And I would be consumed by many questions: What is my life all about? Why am I here, and am I going anywhere when I die? Was life worth it?

But I know where I am going. I know what life is about. The passage of time and the coming of old age do not frighten me because "here we have no lasting city, but we seek the city which is to come" (Heb 13:14).

Thank God that because of Christ I know where I am going and how to get there. If I don't listen to Him, I cannot get there. That is why when I kneel down at night and think of my sins, I change St. Peter's prayer and say: "Lord, do not depart from me, because I am a sinful man. Amen."

WHY BELIEVE IN JESUS CRUCIFIED?

People have asked why anyone would remember Jesus of Nazareth two thousand years after His death. In the eyes of the world He was a misdirected, prophetic young man from the peasant class who offended the authorities of Israel. Even if He offended them for very good reasons, He was considered unwise and therefore died the cruel death of capital punishment. The charge against Him was blasphemy because he had "made Himself the Son of God" (Jn 19:7).

Why would anyone remember Him? This question, while it is rhetorically interesting, betrays a complete lack of appreciation of the history of the early Church. It is true that Jesus of Nazareth did not at first make much impact on world history. His name is first mentioned in secular history only decades after His death, and then His name was misspelled as Crestos. From the Sunday following His death, however, knowledge of Him grew rapidly in Israel and then throughout the Roman Empire. It is possible to trace the development of this knowledge of Him through the Acts of Apostles and the epistles, and especially through the writings of the early Church Fathers: Clement, Ignatius, Justin, and Irenaeus.

Within three hundred years of the coming of Jesus Christ His disciples had transformed the Roman Empire and its treatment of human beings. World history had taken a sharp turn: instead of fighting the barbarians, the Church converted them. By the year 800 one of their descendants, Charlemagne, was crowned emperor of the new (Holy) Roman Empire, which included all of continental Europe.

This amazing transformation, accomplished by a humble carpenter, is one of the great mysteries — perhaps the supreme mystery — of world history, and it happened for only one reason: He was crucified and rose from the dead. The Crucifixion and the Resurrection account for the uniqueness of Christ before the human race. Let us begin with the Crucifixion.

A CRUCIFIED GOD

Because of the innate and God-given religious sensibilities of human beings, religions in the ancient world grew and flourished. Following almost directly from the ancient animist religions came the roots of the Hindu and Taoist religions, characteristic of India and Japan. They came into competition with, and to some degree were overshadowed by, the immense spiritual influence of the Gautama Buddha, who was not a religious founder in a strict sense. He was a moral and ethical philosopher, whose system and teaching brought peace and tranquillity to endless numbers of people. For many reasons his ethical philosophy became enshrined in the Buddhist religion, which has all the characteristics of a world religion despite its pragmatic and philosophical origins. Western people seldom recognize the immense influence of Gautama Buddha, who never claimed any divinity at all and, in fact, considered himself a converted sinner.

The Jewish religion grew out of the interaction of a Bedouin people with the revelations of God to prophetic figures, beginning with Abraham and later Moses. The Jewish leaders spoke to the living God, and they were the people who brought a unique element to world religion. The Jewish religion actually does not fit the definition of a world religion any more than Christianity does, because world religions in many respects are historical and human phenomena. Neither Judaism nor Christianity can be explained within the parameters of the sociology of religion, for neither was of human origin or the product of history.

Christianity has many unique details, the most remarkable of which is that it is the religion of the suffering and dying God. No other religion would present an image of a suffering person, someone who takes on himself the painful realities of human existence. The image of Jesus crucified profoundly moves human beings and catches the attention even of unbelievers. The reaction to the recent film *The Passion of the Christ* is evidence of this. Large numbers of people, including non-Christians, were deeply moved by the film. Others, however, including some Christians, rejected the graphic portrayal of the Gospel narrative of the death of Jesus Christ. We might ask why.

The answer is simply that the idea of a suffering God is very attractive to some and completely repulsive to others. The latter group, if they are Christian, might look to see whether their Christianity has been reduced to a kind of Unitarianism operating under the guise of Christianity. We have to keep in mind that without having a grasp of what Miguel de Unamuno (an unbeliever) called the tragic element of life, we cannot deal with the blood-stained figure of Jesus of Nazareth.

However, if a person has some understanding that Jesus died for us and that His life and terrible death are intended in the divine plan to be part of our salvation, the atonement of our sins, and the example of divine and loving obedience to God, then he will be able to believe in Christ.

Certainly no one would believe in Christ if His death had been the end. He would be yet another tragic figure in human history, a noble hero who attempted to do some good but was destroyed by the evil that haunts human events and whose origins to the unbeliever appear to be quite obscure. If we accept His Resurrection, however, His glorious victory over death, we will see in His face the account of how God saves the world.

Suffering, even when it is acute and terribly unjust, can be the lot of any human being. Those born in the twentieth century, which saw several wars and holocausts and the misuse of technological progress, know only too well that our gadget-filled world has been the scene of stupendous conflicts. In our new century, nations that are being drawn closer by commerce and communication continue to be in conflict, and intelligent people realize that the indescribable horror of a third world war is not a mere fantasy.

Therefore, a belief in Christ's Cross is absolutely necessary. Apart from the international situation, the human potential for acute suffering and physical illness, whether our own or that of a dear one, should make us aware of the tragic element in human existence. At the same time it may make us angry and unbelieving or perhaps deeply resentful and bitterly hostile to God, no matter how He is conceived. In the midst of this is the image of the suffering Jesus of Nazareth, who in the Gospel clearly claims to be one with the Father and promises to draw all men to Himself when He is lifted up (see Jn 12:32). Jesus tells us that He has come not to judge the world but to save it (Jn 12:47), that we may have life more abundantly (Jn 10:10), that He may make all things new (see Rev 21:5), that He will ask the Father to forgive even His bitterest enemies.

The Resurrection of Jesus Christ, as it is proclaimed by the New Testament and the Church

Fathers, is the most remarkable claim ever made by the children of men. It affirms not only that He came back to life but that He came back with an everlasting life, which will not be taken away. It amounts intellectually to the proclamation that from this vast universe of matter a single small particle of matter, a human body, is now enlivened with eternal life. The universe and everything in it move toward an end-time. Nothing that exists in the universe is everlasting, but here is One who has everlasting life.

Taken together with the mystery of the Cross, the glorious Resurrection is both the summit and the great test of faith, as summits test the stamina of mountain climbers. They also represent the highest accomplishment of the mountain climber. The summit of Christianity is the Resurrection. It is the summit of all human belief. Those who have difficulty accepting Christ as a divine person will never be able to approach the mystery of the Resurrection. It may sound like a fable or story or myth of someone who has come back from the dead. That is not what the Gospels report. Christ rose by His own divine power and entered the eternity from which this earthly reality springs.

Can we expect someone living in this era of scientific investigation and endless psychologizing to believe that Christ rose from the dead? If this creed is a true belief in the Resurrection, as taught by the Scriptures and preserved by Church tradition, it should be hard to believe. The only way we can believe it is through the gift of faith.

THE GIFT OF FAITH

As we have indicated already, faith is a decision to believe. Faith can also mean something quite different: an impulse experienced in the human mind and heart to accept what is mysterious and unfathomable. That's what religious faith is, and Christianity leads to the highest possible expression of faith. Martha's words to Jesus at the time of Lazarus' death express that faith and hope: "I know that he will rise again in the resurrection at the last day" (Jn 11:24). To know this, to believe it, to accept it requires the gift of faith and the cultivation of that gift by those who receive it. We will speak more of this in the final chapter.

How do I go about articulating, enriching, and strengthening my commitment to the mystery of God and of Christ? How do I believe? These are questions that follow from "Why do I believe?" But before we get to the next phase of our investigation, we must pause and look at the institution that is divine in its origins but all too human in its membership and operations. That is called the Church, or the community of Christ.

III.

Faith in the Church

In the first two chapters we looked at reasons to believe in God and reasons to believe in Christ, but now we move on to a crucial subject for our times — reasons to believe in the Church.

In a familiar passage in St. Matthew's Gospel, Jesus and the apostles are at a place called Caesarea Philippi — modern Banyas — when Jesus asks them, "Who do men say that the Son of man is?" They gave various answers: John the Baptist, Elijah, Jeremiah. Then Our Lord said, "But who do you say that I am?" And St. Peter replied, "You are the Christ, the Son of the living God." Jesus answered:

> "Blessed are you, Simon Bar-Jonah! For flesh and blood has not revealed this to you, but my Father, who is in heaven. And I tell you, you are Peter, and on this rock I will build my church, and the powers of death shall not prevail against it. I will give you

the keys of the kingdom of heaven, and whatever you bind on earth shall be bound in heaven, and whatever you loose on earth shall be loosed in heaven" (Mt 16:17-19).

A few chapters later Our Lord explains to the apostles about fraternal correction. If someone has sinned, his fault should be pointed out privately and he should be given a chance to make amends. If that does not work, a new tactic must be used.

"But if he does not listen, take one or two others along with you, that every word may be confirmed by the evidence of two or three witnesses. If he refuses to listen to them, tell it to the church; and if he refuses to listen even to the church, let him be to you as a Gentile and a tax collector. Truly, I say to you, whatever you bind on earth shall be bound in heaven, and whatever you loose on earth shall be loosed in heaven" (Mt 18:16-18).

FOUNDED BY CHRIST

Our Lord Jesus Christ founded the Church. The word comes to us from the Greek *kyriakon* and the Latin *ecclesia* and means "calling together of people." It is a group of people gathered out of the multitude.

Those people who say, "I don't need a church" — or "the church" — really do not know much about the New Testament and the Acts of the Apostles. In Acts 5:11 it says, "And great fear came upon the whole church, and upon all who heard of these things." Later, in Acts 8:3, it says, "But Saul laid waste the church, and entering house after house, he dragged off men and women and committed them to prison." There are endless references to the church in the Bible. The word *church* is used at least 77 times in the singular and another 35 times in the plural in the New Testament.

Jesus did not establish a television program. He brought people together. He did not establish a hermitage or a religion where everybody could go into the woods and do their own thing. There are times when I wish He had. Nor did He establish the Quakers. George Fox, a devout Pentecostal man who lived in England in the seventeenth century, founded the Quakers, a religious group without theology, clergy, art, or music. They are a very plain society of good people who pray, mostly in silence, through the intercession of the Holy Spirit, somewhat like a prayer group. In fact, the Quakers call themselves the Society of Friends.

What Our Lord established is a Church — *the* Church. You may get very annoyed with the Church, and you have company. There isn't a priest or bishop in the world who doesn't get annoyed with the Church at times. Even the Pope no doubt gets annoyed by the way members of the Church respond to Christ. The Pope himself, although he may, like John Paul II was, be immensely popular throughout the world as a man of peace, courage, and faith, is frequently criticized. Sadly, most of the criticism comes from members of the Church, people who call themselves Catholics, sometimes even from members of the clergy.

Speaking about the relationship of Christ and the Church, St. Paul says:

> He is the head of the body, the church; he is the beginning, the first-born from the dead, that in everything he might be pre-eminent. For in him all the fulness of God was pleased to dwell, and through him to reconcile to himself all things, whether on earth or in heaven, making peace by the blood of his cross (Col 1:18-20).

NO STRANGERS TO FAILURE AND SCANDAL

Priests celebrate the anniversary of the priesthood every year on Holy Thursday, when Christ instituted the priesthood at the Last Supper. From that beginning what do we witness? The failure of the Church's priests. The apostles, who were the first priests and bishops, failed Christ terribly on the very night of His passion. With one exception they all ran away. Doesn't that tell us something?

At the Last Supper on Holy Thursday, Christ said to Peter, who had been appointed the head of the Church:

> "Satan demanded to have you, that he might sift you like wheat, but I have prayed for you that your faith may not fail; and when you have turned again, strengthen your brethren" (Lk 22:31-32).

Within the next few hours Peter denied Christ three times; fortunately, however, he also regretted that he had failed, and he went off to repent, weeping bitterly.

The Church is a collection of poor sinners. The Catholic Church is a collection of 1.1 billion very poor sinners. That's a lot of original sins, and it is no wonder we have trouble.

If you were to create a bell curve with a statistical sample of 1.1 billion people, you would have at the north end some very holy people like Blessed Teresa of Calcutta and St. Pio of Pietrelcina. At the other end of the bell curve you might find Dracula. They are all there — the good and the bad, the very holy and the very sinful. One modern writer, speaking of the Catholic Church, has written, "Here comes everybody."

Don't be surprised if the Church is well represented in hell. We have been warned by Christ Himself, and in the writings of Sts. Paul, James, and John.

HOW DO WE RESPOND TO THE CHURCH?

St. Paul had his share of fights with members of the early Church. It seems he was often rather perturbed with those he had brought to Christ. He called the Galatians stupid (Gal 3:1). He also had battles with the Corinthians and was annoyed with the Thessalonians. It seems that St. Paul had a short fuse, and he wasn't afraid to let them have it. We read in his second Letter to Timothy that he's all alone. No wonder. Everybody ran away! What is his response to this? Did he quit? Did he write St. Peter a letter and say, "I've had enough. I've had it up to here with all these Christians. I'm quitting"?

No. He sums up his response this way.

> I rejoice in my sufferings for your sake, and in my flesh I complete what is lacking in Christ's afflictions for the sake of his body, that is, the church, of which I became a minister according to the divine office which was given to me for you, to make the word of God fully known, the mystery hidden for ages and generations but now made manifest in his saints (Col 1:24-26).

THE MYSTERY

If there were no Church, there would be limited knowledge or reasonable understanding of the divine mysteries. Among the most important mysteries of the ancient Church, preserved now in the Catholic and Orthodox churches (these two churches were united well into the Middle Ages), are the seven mysteries, or sacraments. These are among Christ's most precious gifts to His Church. These sacred signs, like Baptism and the Eucharist, soon came to be surrounded by deeply meaningful liturgical services, which have survived and grown in beauty over the centuries. This is why Samuel Johnson, who was an Anglican, said, "If a Protestant becomes a Catholic, he gains a lot of things, and if a Catholic becomes a Protestant, he loses a lot of things."

Now, I'm not picking on Protestants. Some of my very best friends are Protestants. My best teachers of the meaning of the Scriptures are the holy black women in Harlem, who belong to churches that are called Protestant because they are not Catholic. They have taught me more about the Bible than anyone else. They breathe the Bible, and I wish they could receive the sacrament of the Holy Eucharist because they certainly outdo the Catholics in reverence.

THE EARLY CHURCH

Some people think that when Our Lord established His Church, it was like the Baptist Church is today. They think the apostles wrote the Bible, and everything was plain and simple, like the Baptist Church. Well, that simply isn't true. The first document written in Christian history after the documents in the New Testament is the Epistle of Clemens Romanus. St. Clement, the bishop of Rome, was the third successor after St. Peter. His epistle can be found in any book of writings of the ancient Church, along with those of the other post-apostolic Church Fathers.[12]

The greatest and most literary of these was Ignatius, bishop of Antioch. He, too, was a successor of St. Peter, but at Antioch, not at Rome. The Church at Antioch had been founded by St. Peter, and it was there that Christ's followers were first called Christians.

When Ignatius was arrested for being a Christian, he, like St. Paul, a Roman citizen, appealed to Caesar, and he, too, was sent to be tried in Rome. Along the way the ship called at several ports on the Mediterranean, where there were small Christian communities. He would give the Christians letters he had written for them and for other churches inland.

One of the churches that St. Ignatius wrote to was at Philadelphia (modern Alasehir, in Turkey). The letter dates from A.D. 105.

> Be careful to observe only one Eucharist, for there is only one flesh of our Lord Jesus Christ and one cup of union with His blood, one altar of sacrifice, as there is only one bishop, with the priests and my fellow servants, the deacons.

Our English word *priest* comes from the Greek *presbyteros* and means elder. St. Ignatius wrote about the Eucharist several times, claiming that when there are no bishops, priests, or deacons, there is no church. This does not sound like the Baptist Church.

As the early Church grew, it did not become a collection of independent churches. It became a united Church held together in persecution by its bishops, many of whom were great men of letters. Among them were the third-century bishops, St. Cyprian of Carthage and St. Irenaeus of Lyon. As time went on and the persecutions came to an end in the fourth century, they were succeeded by the great genius bishops and Church Fathers: Augustine of Hippo, John Chrysostom of Constantinople, and Athanasius of Alexandria, who coined the word Trinity.

One of the ancient churches — the Armenian Apostolic Church — lost track of the other churches. It is located up in the mountains, east of modern Turkey. As one of the archbishops of the Armenian Church, now their Patriarch of Jerusalem, said to me, "It wasn't that we rejected the Council of Chalcedon. We didn't even know it was going on." A Catholic visiting an Armenian church will feel quite at home. Above the altar will be an image of the Blessed Virgin holding the Christ Child. The Armenians, who believe in all the sacraments, have a liturgy that corresponds to our Mass. The head of the Armenian Church is called the *catholicos*. Again, we see the Greek word *catholicos* used in the ancient Church, as it is today, to signify universal, the whole world, the scope of the Church's mission (see Mt 28:19).

THE CATHOLIC CHURCH

I don't like to use the term Roman Catholic, although that is what I am. I belong to the Latin rite of the Roman Catholic Church, but there are millions of Catholics who accept the jurisdiction of the Pope who are not Roman Catholics. Ukrainian Catholics, Ruthenian Catholics, Armenian and Antiochian Catholics, Melkite and Maronite Catholics — all are Catholic and in union with the Pope, but they are not Roman Catholics. The proper name of our Church — the one that is used by the early Church Fathers — is the Catholic Christian Church. My hope is that we will begin to use this term for everyone who accepts the traditional teaching of the early Church and the bishop of Rome as the universal shepherd.

One of the great bishops of the early Church was St. Augustine of Hippo. In the early fifth century Hippo had three bishops at the same time. The Donatists had their bishop. They were a tough, vigilante group who used to beat up Catholics on their way to church. They were holier than the Pope. The Arians, who did not believe in the divinity of Christ or in the Trinity, also had a bishop. St. Augustine, the Catholic bishop of Hippo, wrote to one of the Donatists:

> [T]here are many things to hold me to the Catholic Church, not to speak of her most genuine wisdom, which few spiritual men arrive at understanding in this life, even in a small degree.... The great majority are held most firmly not by a great understanding but by simplicity of faith.... I am held by the one faith of peoples and nations. I am held by the authority nourished on miracles, fostered by hope, increased by charity, strengthened by age. I am held by the episcopal and sacerdotal succession from that very See of Peter the Apostle, to whom after the Resurrection Our Lord committed the charge of feeding His sheep. I am held, in short, by the very name of Catholic, which this Church alone, among so many heresies, has obtained, so that whereas all heretics wish to call themselves Catholic, if a stranger in a place should ask the way to the Catholic Church, no heretic will venture to show him

to his own church or place of meeting. All these cogent reasons, therefore, bind a man who believes in the Catholic Church, even if, owing to the slowness of human reason . . . the truth has not been fully manifested. . . . [N]o one will move me from that faith, which binds my soul with so many close ties to the Christian religion.[13]

Augustine was perhaps the greatest bishop ever ordained in the Catholic Church, at least in the West. Calvin, Luther, and other Protestant theologians who claimed not to have left the Catholic Church constantly quoted from him. Neither Calvin nor Luther would be pleased if they came back and heard people speaking of a Calvinist Church or a Lutheran Church, because neither man thought he could or should start a new church.

MIRACLES

We have already mentioned miracles. The Catholic Church is not bashful about miracles. Anyone who would like to implore a miracle from God can do it very comfortably in the Catholic Church. You can pray to Christ Himself. You can pray at a healing service or at a shrine. You can pray through the intercession of the saints, especially the Blessed Virgin Mary. There is much skepticism today about healings and miracles, so I want to include here a description of a miracle that took place at Lourdes in 1902. A little background on the man to whom we owe this story will be necessary.

Dr. Alexis Carrel (1873–1944) was raised in a devout Catholic family and educated by the Jesuits at Lyon. An uncle was bishop of Clermont-Ferrand. During his years in medical school, however, he became a complete skeptic, following the rationalism of Kant and Auguste Comte. In 1902, Carrel's scientific curiosity about medical healing prompted him to volunteer to accompany a train full of sick pilgrims, many terminally ill, who traveled to Lourdes. One of these was twenty-three-year-old Marie-Louise Bailly, who was in the final stages of tubercular peritonitis. Her abdomen greatly distended, pulse and heartbeat irregular, sedated with morphine because of pain, Marie was close to death when, on the afternoon of May 28, she was taken to the grotto. The nurses and attendants bathed her three times in the waters of the spring. Afterwards Carrel, taking notes all the while, watched Marie lying on her stretcher before the statue of Our Lady in the niche of Massabielle as the pilgrims began the litany of the sick.

Volunteers and stretcher-bearers came crowding in. The little carts were being wheeled from the pools to the grotto.

Lerrac glanced again at Marie Ferrand.[14] Suddenly he stared. It seemed to him that there had been a change, that the harsh shadows on her face had disappeared, that her skin was somehow less ashen.

Surely, he thought, this was a hallucination. But the hallucination itself was interesting psychologically, and might be worth recording.... But if the change in Marie Ferrand was a hallucination, it was the first one Lerrac had ever had. He turned to M.

"Look at our patient again," he said. "Does it seem to you that she has rallied a little?"

"She looks much the same to me," answered M. "All I can see is that she is no worse."

Leaning over the stretcher, Lerrac took her pulse again and listened to her breathing. "The respiration is less rapid," he told M.

"That may mean that she is about to die," said M.

Lerrac made no reply. To him it was obvious that there was a sudden improvement of her general condition. Something was taking place. He stiffened to resist a tremor of emotion. Standing against the low wall near the stretcher, he concentrated all his powers of observation on Marie Ferrand. He did not lift his eyes from her face....

Suddenly Lerrac felt himself turning pale. The blanket which covered Marie Ferrand's distended abdomen was gradually flattening out.

"Look at her abdomen," he exclaimed to M.

"Why, yes ... it seems to have gone down."

The bell of the basilica had just struck three. A few minutes later, there was no longer any sign of distention in Marie Ferrand's abdomen.

Lerrac felt that he was going mad.

Standing beside Marie Ferrand, he watched the intake of her breath and the pulsing at her throat....

This time, for sure, something was taking place.

"How do you feel?" he asked her.

"I feel very well," she answered. "I am still weak, but I feel I have been cured."

There was no longer any doubt: Marie Ferrand's condition was improving so much that she was scarcely recognizable. . . .

Abruptly Lerrac moved off. Making his way through the crowd of pilgrims whose loud prayers he hardly heard, he left the grotto. It was now four o'clock.

A dying girl was recovering.

It was the resurrection of the dead.[15]

Carrel's firsthand account of a miracle, written shortly after his experience at Lourdes in 1902, was not published until 1949, five years after his death. It is interesting to note that while Marie Bailly's cure was immediate and complete (a year later she became a Sister of Charity and nursed the sick for the rest of her life), Carrel's skepticism remained. He went on to a distinguished career, winning the Nobel Prize in medicine for his pioneering work in vascular surgery. For a number of years he was director of the Rockefeller Institute for Medical Research in New York, at the time the most prestigious scientific agency in the world.

He struggled all his life with the problem of knowing God, although he readily accepted His existence and the teachings of the Catholic

Church. In the end he formally returned to the Church and received the last rites.

OUR LORD'S CHURCH

These are some of the Church's treasures: sacraments, Scriptures, devotions, miracles, the love of God and the love of Christ. I am very grateful to God to be a member of this Church. I respect the members of all other churches for their prayer and devotion to Christ. I weep when members of my own Church fail, especially priests, but nothing can change the fact that Jesus said, "On this rock I will build my church" (Mt 16:18).

Because of the Church's wounds many good people have left the Catholic Church to join other churches. At the same time many converts have come into the Catholic Church because they came to believe it is the Church founded by Christ and protected by Him through the ages. Others may call themselves Catholic or Orthodox Christians, or Protestants, but you could never deduce their religion from their behavior. That is the most dangerous situation.

Christ founded the Church because He wanted us to be part of it. Laziness, worldliness, self-indulgence, resentment over neglect, anger over victimization by a representative of the Church — these are not good reasons for not belonging to the Church.

Perhaps my only compelling reason for belonging to the Catholic Christian Church is that Our Lord and Savior Jesus Christ called it His Church and gave His teaching and mysterious sacraments, His own personal ministry, to the Catholic Church. The Church is the field sown with wheat and weeds, of which Our Lord speaks; it is a collection of sinful and repentant apostles, of martyred girls and boys called to be saints, of holy and unholy bishops and popes, of idiots and geniuses, of fervent missionaries and contemplative mystics, of housewives, soldiers, and hoboes who are saints, and of bishops and cardinals who are not. I believe in the Church because Jesus Christ gave it to us in the sorrow of the Last Supper, in the horror of the Crucifixion, and in the glorious light of the Resurrection, when He told Peter to feed His lambs and sheep (see Jn 21).

Romano Guardini, a distinguished theologian before the Second Vatican Council, reminds us that the perfect Church that God intended for the human race was horribly wounded by the fall of Adam and Eve and by the betrayal of Christ during His passion and death. Christ's life and His love for the Church and the human family have revealed that wounded state and made the Church a sign of God's presence in the world — although a wounded one — and a source of salvation for poor sinners.

IV.

How to Grow in Faith

We have discussed belief in God and His revelation, which includes those things contained in what is known as the deposit of faith. This refers to the body of truths revealed by God and taught by the Church. Specifically, we believe in the Catholic faith, which is the oldest expression of the Christian faith. The content of faith grows in this important sense: in the course of time truths are often understood better, seen in a somewhat different light, and can change in order to adjust to that reality.

An example of this is belief in the creation of the world. In ancient times, when people had no knowledge of the age of the earth, they readily accepted the apparent biblical chronology, which made the world about six thousand years old. People such as St. Augustine suspected that it was much older and that the days referred to in the creation account in the book of Genesis did not necessarily mean a twenty-four-hour cycle.

In one place St. Augustine seems to suggest that the world could possibly be three billion years old. In modern times, as astronomy and prehistory have become better understood, we have no problem adjusting the understanding of our faith to new dimensions of time and space. In fact, the acknowledgment that the world is so ancient and the universe so huge makes the content of the faith even more enriched and fascinating.

THE ACT OF FAITH

When we speak of faith or believing, we generally mean an action of the will, a decision to accept what faith teaches and what goes beyond human comprehension. We do not do this blindly; we are guided by Scripture and the traditional teachings of the ancient Church, which are interpretations of Scripture. We make an act of faith to believe that Jesus Christ is the Son of God. We also believe that He is a divine person, who at a certain moment of time assumed human nature, including a human body and a human soul. This fact, incomprehensible by human reason alone, is revealed by the New Testament, and its interpretation has been given by the early ecumenical councils of the Church. By an act of faith we accept many things that are not explicitly in the Bible, for example, the doctrine of the most Holy Trinity. The word *trinity* is not mentioned in the Bible but was coined by the council fathers at Nicea (A.D. 325), probably by St. Athanasius. It combines two words, *tri* and *unitas*, meaning a unity of three. When we accept the Holy Trinity, we make an act of faith. We decide to accept God's revelation and the Church's interpretation, and that becomes our act of faith.

Like any human act, faith can be subject to the vicissitudes of our lives. One day we may be very fervent and deeply impressed by some religious idea or event; on another day we may be depressed and everything may seem bleak and meaningless. However, a strong act of faith takes us through good times and bad.

THE GRACE OF FAITH

Faith can be sustained in dark times because in addition to being an act of the human being, it is a gift of God. We cannot believe truly in God's mysteries and what He has revealed unless He gives the grace, or gift, to do so. Unfortunately, people have grown ignorant of the gift of faith and the idea of grace; consequently, they are easy prey to the winds of change and their own psychological moods. Most of us received the gift of faith through the instrumentality of family and parents. Others have received the gift through the study of Scripture and the early Church. Still others have almost stumbled on faith, like St. Paul. God had been waiting for them somewhere along the road. On one day they may dismiss the whole idea of religion and Christianity, and the next day something calls to them in their inmost being and they begin to believe. As St. Augustine says, "With an unheard voice you called to me." However faith is obtained, it should be cherished, since its effects make it a gift of immense value.

Without faith we have no hope, and life becomes a meaningless drudgery, a frenetic pursuit of pleasure. Time is always running out for everyone. Those who derive their meaning as human beings or the meaning of their life from this world will see eventually that they have been betrayed. They may fail, grow ill, be falsely accused of a crime, or undergo financial reverses. Even if they manage to avoid all of these, they will one day grow old and become dependent on others for their care as they await death. The believer seldom has any perception of how dreadful life must be without faith. At the same time the unbeliever who scoffs at faith may be trapped in his own search for meaning. Some unbelievers openly admit that they wish they had faith. Others take refuge in laughing at what they do not have or cannot appreciate.

If we stand back from the beautiful idea of faith and belief, we can see that we have to work at it. Faith does not just happen. It may have been given to someone as a child, but it will not be sustained unless it is cherished and taken care of.

FAITH: DIFFERENT KINDS AND DIFFERENT RESPONSIBILITIES

Faith is manifest in many ways. First, there is the simple faith of a child, which may continue as the simple faith of an adult. Even unbelievers find such faith moving, and it has been portrayed in art, as in Millet's painting of the two laborers who pause in the field to say the Angelus and in the works of Henry Tanner depicting the faith of humble believers, especially African Americans.

It is a strange paradox that simple faith may also be an embarrassment to more sophisticated believers. As children, they may have had a simple faith themselves; but now that they have become educated — in whatever sense that word may be taken — they will look down on, possibly even despise, the simple expression of faith of humble people. They may smirk or laugh, and this reveals a very unhealthy state of affairs. Christ tells us that unless we have faith like a child's, we shall not enter the kingdom of heaven. Christ was very clear about His high regard for simple faith. "And calling to him a child, he put him in the midst of them, and said, 'Truly, I say to you, unless you turn and become like children, you will never enter the kingdom of heaven'" (Mt 18: 2-3).

CHALLENGED FAITH

For a great many people the contents of faith, accepted in childhood, become challenged as the years go on. Naturally and unavoidably, children must be told things with simple comparisons and analogues. Before the age of eleven, when children normally begin the process of abstract thinking, they picture God as an old man with a white beard and a few angels behind Him. As they move into adolescence, the thought of God as a pure spirit may begin to dawn on them, and they may be receptive to the mystery of the Incarnation — God becoming a human being. This can be very challenging.

One of the most frequent sources of challenge comes from science, as it is understood by people in school or by those who have seriously pursued the study of the material universe. Someone who understands what divine revelation is and the limits of natural science, whether one is a believer or not, realizes that scientific knowledge cannot challenge these beliefs. For instance, science, which pertains to the physical and measurable exclusively, can neither affirm nor deny God's existence. Science and the knowledge obtained from it may present the believer with marvelous opportunities to expand faith, as with the astronomical discoveries of the twentieth century, and leave us awestruck by the size of God's creation.

On the other hand, the same facts will challenge the previous naïve perceptions of the universe, which were shared by both scientists and religious people. In claiming that there is no battle between science and faith, we are saying something profound. Those who do not think profoundly, however, will not comprehend this fact. It is possible and enriching to follow the paths of science on the one hand, and faith and revelation on the other, and see how they relate but do not contradict each other, since they examine reality from different points of view. Thus we see great figures in science who have faith, and religious people who feel quite at home in the world of science.

When science is abused to contradict faith, it is usually presented in one of two ways. It is a poorly understood use of science, which is often unavoidable because of a person's level of education. This happens with high school science textbooks, which frequently lack competence to challenge religious ideas intelligently. It is understandable but unintelligent that religious convictions are used to challenge science by those who feel they have been taken advantage of unfairly. The education wars in the United States between those who accept the *theory* of evolution and those who literally interpret the accounts of creation in Sacred Scripture are founded on a misunderstanding of science and faith. A great deal of energy is expended, unfortunately, on what is basically a misunderstanding.

In a second and more sophisticated way, science may also challenge religious faith by giving a person a single way of looking at reality. Many scientists end up by being materialists, that is, they jump from the study of material things to the unwarranted conclusion that all of reality is material. Actually, human beings do not even entirely understand what the word *material* means. Nor do we have full comprehension of the supernatural, since we do not understand all that is meant by the word *natural*. A person caught in this misunderstanding will be stunted. Many scientists have worked hard to escape the narrow prejudice of scientific materialism, which is different from science itself. Dr. Alexis Carrel, whom we have already mentioned, exemplifies this coming together of science and faith. It is important, however, that the believer understand that the realities represented by faith existed long before the material and will continue long after it.

Other things in life, like tragedy or adversity, present challenges to our faith. Disaster occurs to many, including those who believe in a personal God and His Providence. When there is death, especially of a dear one, or a natural calamity, like a tidal wave, the question is asked: Where is God in all of this? Out of such situations can come a deeper understanding of faith, an escape from those touching but incomplete estimations of God and His Providence that are characteristic of children and simple people. When we are faced with tragedy, even terminal illness, if we are willing through prayer to work with the gift of faith in the darkness, peace and acceptance can be found.

In order to pass successfully through personal tragedy or some physical or moral evil, much prayer will be needed if faith is not to be lost. St. Thomas observed that for most people belief or nonbelief in God can be traced to the problem of evil; the believer finds in God an understanding of the problem, and the unbeliever sees evil only as an enigma.

Regardless of what has been thought in the past, unbelievers are often not people of ill will. The believer so easily assumes that they are. We have to remember that many people have as yet not received the gift of faith. I would like to believe that everyone is at some time offered the gift, but it may come only at the moment of death. Without faith there is no hope of eternal life.

Most of us have known good people who were either agnostic (they were not sure about God's existence) or atheists (they could not find in their experience any comprehension of faith or the ability to ask for it). Believers are well advised not to judge others, as Christ warns us (see Mt 7:1). Unbelievers may be dealing with conflicts, problems, or other negative experiences in their past. We should be understanding of this.

The following poem by an unbeliever reveals to the sympathetic believer how a person can reach the point of being an atheist.

The Atheist's Prayer

Hear my petition, you God who do not exist
And into your nothingness gather these my
*   griefs again*
You who never abandoned unhappy men
Without the consolation of illusion. Do not
*   resist*
Our petition; may our longing by you be
*   dressed.*
When you remove yourself furthest from my
*   sight,*
The fairy-tales to sweeten my sad night
Told by my soul, I then remember best.
How great you are, my God! So great you are
That you are not, except as an idea.
How narrow the reality, though it expands so
*   far*
In order to include you. I suffer from your mere
Non-existence, God, since if it were that you
Were to exist, then I would really too.[16]

Unamuno, who tried always to be honest, acknowledges at the end of his prayer not so much atheism as agnosticism, and his agnosticism is more a problem of himself than of God's existence. He had such a profound appreciation of the tragic element in human existence that he found it difficult to believe that he was real himself. The core issues here, as in many cases of unbelief, are with the individual, not with God.

There are also challenges to particular expressions of faith. Devout members of the various denominations and movements of Christianity may suddenly "discover" that their heretofore acceptance of a particular belief is apparently unwarranted by Sacred Scripture or by ancient Church tradition. They are thereby put into conflict with the content of the faith. This is how it comes about that there are religious converts within Christianity and people moving from one church to another.

When people tell me they have left the Catholic faith and enumerate their reasons, it is often obvious that they have misunderstood faith in the first place. Their ignorance may be quite blameless since the faith is frequently not well taught, particularly at the present time. They may have experienced a burst of fervor and subsequently found the local representation of Catholic Christianity lukewarm and unattractive.

I can think of a man I know who was a tepid Catholic, faced a crisis, and was helped by some evangelical Protestants. He went from being a non-practicing Catholic to a fervent Evangelical. One day, as he was examining the teachings of the Catholic Church in order to be able to refute them, he began to see how closely they followed Sacred Scripture. As a result, he transferred his fervor and devotion back to the Church he had come from. What do we say of this type of experience of faith? We must allow God to lead people, even if they make what seems to be a wrong turn on the road. It is certainly true that a fervent Evangelical is more capable of pleasing God than someone who is a lukewarm member of some other group, even of the Catholic Church.

Sustaining and Growing in Faith

People experience two distinct challenges to faith, the origins of which we have already described. The main challenge is to sustain faith against the things that would undermine it and to grow in faith.

Sustaining faith that is under attack from skepticism or from trials of discouragement is a matter of the will interacting with divine grace. The worst thing to do in such a situation is to engage in internal arguments pro and con.

Because faith is a positive decision, people all too easily relinquish their determination and give in to negativism. This may not lead to doubting everything about faith, but it does engage them in negative ideas and thinking, which become a dialogue of doubt.

With internal monologues there is no opportunity for someone else to participate. The believer hesitates to include another person in what is so uncomfortable a situation. The internal monologues often have a good deal of anger aimed at God. Since no good Christian wants to be angry with God, the anger is denied. It builds up, however, as a negative feeling and can go on for days, weeks, or months. The negative dialogue must be recognized and resolved. Negativism does not work, although it may be perfectly excusable. A victim of a stroke or other serious illness may easily entertain ideas against the Providence of God and faith itself. From asking the question, "Why did God let this happen?" we may move to, "Is there a God who let it happen?" This dialogue is not helpful, because it is fueled by depression and perhaps desperation. It can darken someone's whole experience of life. Things that might strengthen faith will be rejected out of hand. Prayer, in particular, will evaporate or become very brief and rather desperate and conflicted.

People in Alcoholics Anonymous refer to this type of experience as "stinking thinking." It's not a bad phrase. Whereas the believer may be willing to accept that a person subject to addiction may be prey to this kind of thinking, the believer is likely to dismiss this possibility in his own life. This negative thinking is one of the real challenges to faith.

If someone needs to share their troubles and rising doubts, it is wise to do so with a person who is at home with and firm in their faith, yet at the same time sympathetic and understanding. The best person is someone who has lived through dark times and can recognize the symptoms of bad thinking. Personal guilt about our bad thinking is not at all helpful, because it will only add to the guilt and angry relationship with God. The first step in dealing with problems of faith is to recognize and get the trial out into the open.

The second step is to pray. Prayer is always a possibility, even in the midst of deep depression and confusion. We sometimes think prayer is not possible, because distraction makes it more difficult to focus our prayer or because we have no taste for what is generally thought of as prayer.

At the end of this book we will include some thoughts for people struggling with faith. They may not be struggling with doubt but with misunderstanding, lack of comprehension, and mindsets that do not accept God's authority.

The prayer of someone struggling with faith can, in retrospect, be very beautiful. It can represent loyalty to God in the most adverse circumstances, but it will not seem to be anything so positive while it is going on. The prayer will seem rather to possess a desperate quality; there will at least be many temptations to give up prayer.

It is not unreasonable or ill-advised to introduce the idea of temptations against faith that may come from other sources. Modern people do not like to engage the idea of the diabolical. However, our struggles, as we know from St. Paul, are "against the principalities, against the powers, against the world rulers of this present darkness" (Eph 6:12). An immense amount of damage in human affairs and in the life of the Church is caused by temptations and trials that come from outside an individual. A form of modern skepticism denies that such temptations could originate outside the individual, or at least outside the general thinking of human beings. In fact, an objective reading of even a concise history of the twentieth century reveals to the open-minded reader not only the possibility of diabolical intrusion into human affairs, but the conviction that we are often harmed by forces beyond us. Both Bolshevik Communism and Nazism are filled with such appalling violence and evil that they provide a powerful motivation for taking the diabolical seriously.

I once read the final words of Lenin, the Communist tyrant, who lamented the ocean of blood he had shed. If he had had ten men working with him like St. Francis, he said, he could have saved Russia. Most people would say that Lenin had done the work of Satan, but something in him still made him think of the gentle saint.

It is not necessary to confront the diabolical directly; in fact, it may not be a good idea to do so. We have to be aware, however, that among the array of forces lined up against our faith, the diabolical is a key player.

Prayer in dark times should be quiet and simple: "Oh, Lord, I believe; help my unbelief." How simple and powerful is this prayer. It is so much more effective to pray for light and guidance during dark times than it is to engage in the internal monologue with oneself, arguing the pros and cons of belief. In psychology it is said that important life decisions should not be made at a time of crisis or depression. A corollary of this should be that decisions about our relationship with God should not be made when things are going badly.

Sustaining Faith in Good Times

Apart from challenges to faith, there is the work of sustaining faith. Among other things, faith is a human experience with profound psychological components. Psychology has shown that the way to strengthen or grow in any trait or inner conviction is to respond to it positively. If we do not embrace faith and respond to it positively, it will wither away. By distracting us with worldly goals, secularism undermines faith. A family that has usually gone to Mass on Sunday may find more and more excuses for not going. The lame excuse, "I did not feel like it," will begin to affect the rest of a person's life. Attendance at Mass may become a monthly or semiannual event. If children experience no positive affirmation of faith in the home, they will drift further away from the Church.

If faith is not to die, it must be cultivated and strengthened by the daily practice of prayer and virtuous deeds. It is interesting to observe that in unbelieving times when faith is attacked and even persecuted, families and individuals who practice their faith may actually be growing in it. Many people in secular society manifest deep religious faith and evaluate the events of life from the perspective of faith. At the same time there are in the same household or on the same block people for whom faith has become a distant memory, nostalgia for things past, or perhaps something from their earlier lives that they now resent. Growing in faith means doing the things of faith. When we say the Creed and meditate on its contents and are willing to make logical and coherent decisions that faith demands, we will grow in faith.

There are a number of issues in contemporary society on which the teachings of faith are manifestly clear. The absolute sinfulness of destroying an innocent human life is so obvious that people must lie to themselves in order to defend such a procedure. Nonetheless, for a variety of reasons believers will do so. They have to know, however, that they are undermining their own faith. If they can thus violate one of God's commandments quietly and calmly, it will soon become easy to violate others. The secular world spends a great deal of time and energy trying to justify the denial of the truths of faith. People put a nice face on murder, infanticide, and other behaviors that are clearly contrary to the teachings of faith. At the same time, they try to persuade us that the viewpoint of the unbelieving world is as virtuous as that of the believer, or perhaps more so. An amazing number of people accept this, including faculty members of Catholic universities and perhaps even the spokesmen of dioceses. We undermine and sometimes lose our faith when we embrace what is, in origin, selfish, pagan, or even diabolical. How faith is strengthened when we assert ourselves against these forces! It takes a great effort, however, because the forces of unbelief and immorality find a welcome home in our hearts, which have been deeply scarred by original sin. It is easy to forget that even if we have been baptized and have tried to live a life of grace, the lasting effects of original sin — the darkening of the intellect, the weakening of the will, and the corruption of human relationships — remain in us and must be dealt with effectively through constant prayer and repentance throughout life.

WORKS OF FAITH

One of the best ways to deal with doubt and strengthen our faith is to do things that have no earthly use to us but which give honor and glory to God. It may be something simple, like giving an alms to an unknown person, or it may be something quite painful, like accepting insult or abuse without protest. It may be something on a larger scale, like making a significant sacrifice for what we believe. Many people have lost jobs or friends because they stood up for something that faith told them to defend or protest. One of the best things I ever did for my faith was voluntarily go to jail for a short time for having said a Rosary in front of an abortion clinic. I did not like the idea of going to jail, and when I got there it was not a good experience. It was not something to be taken lightly, but it did have some positive results. I didn't even have my office book with me, but the guard kindly let me keep my New Testament. I read, as I had never read before, whole books of the New Testament. They were more real to me than they had ever been. It was a time of faith.

Many times we do religious things that are not only pleasant but also ego-enhancing. Belonging to the Church or to the clergy can be a bit of an ego trip, but if we perform the works of faith at a cost to ourselves — if we are ignored or insulted or inconvenienced — then we are strengthening our faith. At a time in history when faith is shallow among so many, it is a good idea to look for opportunities to show our faith quietly and humbly, in ways that will cost us, and thereby make an emotional investment in what we profess to believe.

The works of faith can also be long-range and humdrum. St. Thérèse of Lisieux once said to one of her sisters, "I prefer the monotony of sacrifice to any ecstasy." She experienced much of the monotony of sacrifice during her short life. People often give decades of time, or even their whole lives, to do something that does not interest them or that they would not have chosen to do. This is an example of doing a work of faith.

Sister Anastasia, a sage and elderly member of the Carmelite Sisters of the Sacred Heart of Alhambra, California, has observed, "It's not a sacrifice unless it stings." We should examine our lives to see what manifestation there is of faith and the love of God that "stings." This is how we grow.

THE PRAYERS OF FAITH

The prayers of faith are much the same as the works. They are prayers we say with a sense of duty and responsibility, even when we find them boring. There is probably no better example than the Rosary or the Divine Mercy chaplet. Those who make these devotions part of their daily prayer in season and out of season, whether they feel well or ill, will know true growth in faith and devotion. The idea has come about in our time that in order to pray successfully in church, we must be amused and entertained by beautiful music or some other distraction. That attitude leaves little room for the prayers of faith, which are insistent and performed in spite of personal feelings or emotions. Of course, we should lift up our minds and inspire our hearts by good prayer, but when that kind of prayer is not available and we go on in the darkness, that is when we grow in faith.

Mother Teresa of Calcutta was one of the great people of faith in our time. On the one hand, she said she could not experience faith, hope, or love, that everything was empty and dark, and that her prayers fell back on her like sharp knives to wound her. On the other hand, she went on with great faith, hope, and love — not feeling them but determined to persevere. There is probably no better example in modern times of someone of immense faith who received little personal reinforcement. She did not look for any, nor did she buckle when she did not receive any. During the process of Mother Teresa's beatification, her spiritual directors were required to make public her personal notes, which revealed her years of spiritual thirst and darkness.

People often ask why someone like Mother Teresa experienced spiritual darkness for nearly thirty-five years. She asked the same question in some of her prayers: "Lord, what do you get out of this?" In fact, she became the great believer of the twentieth century. When she spoke at the United Nations, the Secretary-General remarked that from the podium of the General Assembly the world's most powerful men had spoken. He introduced her by saying, "Now we hear from the most powerful woman in the world."

How does someone become so powerful? By works of faith, by going on in season and out of season, by accepting darkness when God sends it. That is what we must do on our journey to eternal life.

The best prayers of faith are said in times of difficulty and darkness. They give us the opportunity not only to bend our wills to follow God but also to struggle to receive His grace. They make us humble in the presence of the Holy Trinity because they make clear how dependent we are on God's grace to make any progress in the spiritual life. Perhaps some of the best prayers of faith we have ever said have been uttered in times of desperation and tragedy. However, gentle and devout prayers of thanksgiving are needed when we are feeling well. At that point we have the tranquillity of prayer, which is also important.

We live in times filled with challenges to faith from the media, from Catholics who are losing or have lost their faith, and from many outside forces. To pray in each of these circumstances is to exercise and grow in faith. No one should think that faith is easy.

It is important to be informed of the truths of faith. This is why the Creed is so important. In the last section of the book we will include the Creed of the People of God, composed by Pope Paul VI in 1968. It was extremely necessary at the time because of a good deal of theological confusion in the Church. Unfortunately, it did not abate in the next decades. The 1970s and 1980s were filled with more confusion. Now, as we try to rebuild faith after the long pontificate of John Paul II and in the light of the powerful faith of Pope Benedict XVI, we should meditate on the Creed of the People of God as well as on other teachings and examples of faith. The profound experience of darkness of St. Thérèse at her decision to believe should teach us much.

APPENDICES

Appendix A

The New Testament Teaching on Faith

There are a great many passages from the Gospels and epistles on faith and the nature of faith. We have selected only a few to be considered here for your meditation.

"For now we see in a mirror dimly, but then face to face. Now I know in part; then I shall understand fully, even as I have been fully understood" (1 Cor 13:12).

"For this reason, because I have heard of your faith in the Lord Jesus and your love toward all the saints, I do not cease to give thanks for you, remembering you in my prayers, that the God of our Lord Jesus Christ, the Father of glory, may give you a spirit of wisdom and of revelation in the knowledge of him, having the eyes of your hearts enlightened, that you may know what is the hope to which he has called you, what are the riches of his glorious inheritance in the saints, and what is the immeasurable greatness of his power in us who believe, according to the working of his great might" (Eph 1:15-19).

"Now faith is the assurance of things hoped for, the conviction of things not seen" (Heb 11:1).

"We heard this voice borne from heaven, for we were with him on the holy mountain. And we have the prophetic word made more sure. You will do well to pay attention to this as to a lamp shining in a dark place, until the day dawns and the morning star rises in your hearts" (2 Pet 1:18-19).

"There is one body and one Spirit, just as you were called to the one hope that belongs to your call, one Lord, one faith, one baptism" (Eph 4:4-5).

"And without faith it is impossible to please him. For whoever would draw near to God must believe that he exists and that he rewards those who seek him" (Heb 11:6).

"But to all who received him, who believed in his name, he gave power to become children of God" (Jn 1:12).

"For God so loved the world that he gave his only Son, that whoever believes in him should not perish but have eternal life" (Jn 3:16).

"Jesus said to them, 'I am the bread of life; he who comes to me shall not hunger, and he who believes in me shall never thirst'" (Jn 6:35).

"For whoever is ashamed of me and of my words, of him will the Son of man be ashamed when he comes in his glory and the glory of the Father and of the holy angels" (Lk 9:26).

"Then Jesus answered her, 'O woman, great is your faith! Be it done for you as you desire'" (Mt 15:28).

"What does it profit, my brethren, if a man says he has faith but has not works? Can his faith save him? If a brother or sister is ill-clad and in lack of daily food, and one of you says to them, 'Go in peace, be warmed and filled,' without giving them the things needed for the body, what does it profit? So faith by itself, if it has no works, is dead.

But some one will say, 'You have faith and I have works.' Show me your faith apart from your works, and I by my works will show you my faith" (Jas 2:14-18).

Appendix B

Credo of the People of God

**Proclaimed by His Holiness,
Pope Paul VI, on June 30, 1968**

We believe in one only God, Father, Son, and Holy Spirit, creator of things visible such as this world in which our transient life passes, of things invisible such as the pure spirits which are also called angels, and creator in each man of his spiritual and immortal soul.

We believe that this only God is absolutely one in His infinitely holy essence as also in all His perfections, in His omnipotence, His infinite knowledge, His providence, His will and His love. He is He who is, as He revealed to Moses, and He is love, as the apostle John teaches us: so that these two names, being and love, express ineffably the same divine reality of Him who has wished to make Himself known to us, and who, "dwelling in light inaccessible" is in Himself above every name, above every thing and above every created intellect. God alone can give us right and full knowledge of this reality by revealing Himself as Father, Son, and Holy Spirit, in whose eternal life we are by grace called to share, here below in the obscurity of faith and after death in eternal light. The mutual bonds which eternally constitute the Three Persons, who are each one and the same divine being, are the blessed inmost life of God thrice holy, infinitely beyond all that we can conceive in human measure. We give thanks, however, to the divine goodness that very many believers can testify with us before men to the unity of God, even though they know not the mystery of the most Holy Trinity.

We believe then in the Father who eternally begets the Son, in the Son, the Word of God, who is eternally begotten; in the Holy Spirit, the uncreated Person who proceeds from the Father and the Son as their eternal love. Thus in the Three Divine Persons, coeternal and coequal, the life and beatitude of God, perfectly one, superabound and are consummated in the supreme excellence and glory proper to uncreated being, and always "there should be venerated unity in the Trinity and Trinity in the unity."

We believe in our Lord Jesus Christ, who is the Son of God. He is the Eternal Word, born of the Father before time began, and one in substance with the Father, and through Him all things were made. He was incarnate of the Virgin Mary by the power of the Holy Spirit, and was made man: equal therefore to the Father according to His divinity, and inferior to the Father according to His humanity; and Himself one, not by some impossible confusion of His natures, but by the unity of His person.

He dwelt among us, full of grace and truth. He proclaimed and established the Kingdom of God and made us know in Himself the Father. He gave us His new commandment to love one another as He loved us. He taught us the way of the beatitudes of the Gospel: poverty in spirit, meekness, suffering borne with patience, thirst after justice, mercy, purity of heart, will for peace, persecution suffered for justice sake. Under Pontius Pilate He suffered — the Lamb of God bearing on Himself the sins of the world, and He died for us on the cross, saving us by His redeeming blood. He was buried, and, of His own power, rose on the third day, raising us by His resurrection to that sharing in the divine life which is the life of grace. He ascended to heaven, and He will come again, this time in glory, to judge the living and the dead: each according to his merits — those who have responded to the love and piety of God going to eternal life, those who have refused them to the end going to the fire that is not extinguished.

And His Kingdom will have no end.

We believe in the Holy Spirit, who is Lord, and Giver of life, who is adored and glorified together with the Father and the Son. He spoke to us by the prophets; He was sent by Christ after His resurrection and His ascension to the Father; He illuminates, vivifies, protects and guides the Church; He purifies the Church's members if they do not shun His grace. His action, which penetrates to the inmost of the soul, enables man to respond to the call of Jesus: Be perfect as your Heavenly Father is perfect (Mt 5:48).

We believe that Mary is the Mother, who remained ever a Virgin, of the Incarnate Word, our God and Savior Jesus Christ, and that by reason of this singular election, she was, in consideration of the merits of her Son, redeemed in a more eminent manner, preserved from all stain of original sin and filled with the gift of grace more than all other creatures.

Joined by a close and indissoluble bond to the Mysteries of the Incarnation and Redemption, the Blessed Virgin, the Immaculate, was at the end of her earthly life raised body and soul to heavenly glory and likened to her risen Son in anticipation of the future lot of all the just; and we believe that the Blessed Mother of God, the New Eve, Mother of the Church, continues in heaven her maternal role with regard to Christ's members, cooperating with the birth and growth of divine life in the souls of the redeemed.

We believe that in Adam all have sinned, which means that the original offense committed by him caused human nature, common to all, to fall to a state in which it bears the consequences of that offense, and which is not the state in which it was at first in our first parents — established as they were in holiness and justice, and in which they knew neither evil nor death. It is human nature so fallen stripped of the grace that clothed it, injured in its own natural powers and subjected to the dominion of death, that is transmitted to all, and it is in this sense that everyone is born in sin. We therefore hold, with the Council of Trent, that original sin, is transmitted with human nature, "not by imitation, but by propagation" and that it is thus "proper to everyone."

We believe that Our Lord Jesus Christ, by the sacrifice of the cross redeemed us from original sin and all the personal sins committed by each one of us, so that, in accordance with the word of the apostle, "where sin abounded grace did more abound."

We believe in one Baptism instituted by our Lord Jesus Christ for the remission of sins. Baptism should be administered even to little children who have not yet been able to be guilty of any personal sin, in order that, though born deprived of supernatural grace, they may be reborn "of water and the Holy Spirit" to the divine life in Christ Jesus.

We believe in one, holy, catholic, and apostolic Church built by Jesus Christ on that rock which is Peter. She is the Mystical Body of Christ; at the same time a visible society instituted with hierarchical organs, and a spiritual community; the Church on earth, the pilgrim People of God here below, and the Church filled with heavenly blessings; the germ and the first fruits of the Kingdom of God, through which the work and the sufferings of Redemption are continued throughout human history, and which looks for its perfect accomplishment beyond time in glory. In the course of time, the Lord Jesus forms His Church by means of the sacraments emanating from His plenitude. By these she makes her members participants in the Mystery of the Death and Resurrection of Christ, in the grace of the Holy Spirit who gives her life and movement. She is therefore holy, though she has sinners in her bosom, because she herself has no other life but that of grace: it is by living by her life that her members are sanctified; it is by removing themselves from her life that they fall into sins and disorders that prevent the radiation of her sanctity. This is why she suffers and does penance for these offenses, of which she has the power to heal her children through the blood of Christ and the gift of the Holy Spirit.

Heiress of the divine promises and daughter of Abraham according to the Spirit, through that Israel whose scriptures she lovingly guards, and whose patriarchs and prophets she venerates; founded upon the apostles and handing on from century to century their ever-living word and their powers as pastors in the successor of Peter and the bishops in communion with him; perpetually assisted by the Holy Spirit, she has the charge of guarding, teaching, explaining and spreading the Truth which God revealed in a then veiled manner by the prophets, and fully by the Lord Jesus. We believe all that is contained in the word of God written or handed down, and that the Church proposes for belief as divinely revealed, whether by a solemn judgment or by the ordinary and universal magisterium. We believe in the infallibility enjoyed by the successor of Peter when he teaches ex cathedra as pastor and teacher of all the faithful, and which is assured also to the episcopal body when it exercises with him the supreme magisterium.

We believe that the Church founded by Jesus Christ and for which He prayed is indefectibly one in faith, worship and the bond of hierarchical communion. In the bosom of this Church, the rich variety of liturgical rites and the legitimate diversity of theological and spiritual heritages and special disciplines, far from injuring her unity, make it more manifest.

Recognizing also the existence, outside the organism of the Church of Christ of numerous elements of truth and sanctification which belong to her as her own and tend to Catholic unity, and believing in the action of the Holy Spirit who stirs up in the heart of the disciples of Christ love of this unity, we entertain the hope that the Christians who are not yet in the full communion of the one only Church will one day be reunited in one flock with one only shepherd.

We believe that the Church is necessary for salvation, because Christ, who is the sole mediator and way of salvation, renders Himself present for us in His body which is the Church. But the divine design of salvation embraces all, and those who without fault on their part do not know the Gospel of Christ and His Church, but seek God sincerely, and under the influence of grace endeavor to do His will as recognized through the promptings of their conscience, they, in a number known only to God, can obtain salvation.

We believe that the Mass, celebrated by the priest representing the person of Christ by virtue of the power received through the Sacrament of Orders, and offered by him in the name of Christ and the members of His Mystical Body, is the sacrifice of Calvary rendered sacramentally present on our altars. We believe that as the bread and wine consecrated by the Lord at the Last Supper were changed into His body and His blood which were to be offered for us on the cross, likewise the bread and wine consecrated by the priest are changed into the body and blood of Christ enthroned gloriously in heaven, and we believe that the mysterious presence of the Lord, under what continues to appear to our senses as before, is a true, real and substantial presence.

Christ cannot be thus present in this sacrament except by the change into His body of the reality itself of the bread and the change into His blood of the reality itself of the wine, leaving unchanged only the properties of the bread and wine which our senses perceive. This mysterious change is very appropriately called by the Church transubstantiation. Every theological explanation which seeks some understanding of this mystery must, in order to be in accord with Catholic faith, maintain that in the reality itself, independently of our mind, the bread and wine have ceased to exist after the Consecration, so that it is the adorable body and blood of the Lord Jesus that from then on are really before us under the sacramental species of bread and wine, as the Lord willed it, in order to give Himself to us as food and to associate us with the unity of His Mystical Body.

The unique and indivisible existence of the Lord glorious in heaven is not multiplied, but is rendered present by the sacrament in the many places on earth where Mass is celebrated. And this existence remains present, after the sacrifice, in the Blessed Sacrament which is, in the tabernacle, the living heart of each of our churches. And it is our very sweet duty to honor and adore in the blessed Host which our eyes see, the Incarnate Word whom they cannot see, and who, without leaving heaven, is made present before us.

We confess that the Kingdom of God begun here below in the Church of Christ is not of this world whose form is passing, and that its proper growth cannot be confounded with the progress of civilization, of science or of human technology, but that it consists in an ever more profound knowledge of the unfathomable riches of Christ, an ever stronger hope in eternal blessings, an ever more ardent response to the love of God, and an ever more generous bestowal of grace and holiness among human beings. But it is this same love which induces the Church to concern herself constantly about the true temporal welfare of the human race. Without ceasing to recall to her children that they have not here a lasting dwelling, she also urges them to contribute, each according to his vocation and his means, to the welfare of their earthly city, to promote justice, peace and brotherhood among men and women, to give their aid freely to their brothers and sisters, especially to the poorest and most unfortunate. The deep solicitude of the Church, the Spouse of Christ, for the needs of human beings, for their joys and hopes, their griefs and efforts, is therefore nothing other than her great desire to be present to them, in order to illuminate them with the light of Christ and to gather them all in Him, their only Savior. This solicitude can never mean that the Church conform herself to the things of this world, or that she lessen the ardor of her expectation of her Lord and of the eternal Kingdom.

We believe in the life eternal. We believe that the souls of all those who die in the grace of Christ — whether they must still be purified in purgatory, or whether from the moment they leave their bodies Jesus takes them to paradise as He did for the Good Thief — are the People of God in the eternity beyond death, which will be finally conquered on the day of the Resurrection when these souls will be reunited with their bodies.

We believe that the multitude of those gathered around Jesus and Mary in paradise forms the Church of Heaven, where in eternal beatitude they see God as He is, and where they also, in different degrees, are associated with the holy angels in the divine rule exercised by Christ in glory, interceding for us and helping our weakness by their brotherly care.

We believe in the communion of all the faithful of Christ, those who are pilgrims on earth, the dead who are attaining their purification, and the blessed in heaven, all together forming one Church; and we believe that in this communion the merciful love of God and His saints is ever listening to our prayers, as Jesus told us: Ask and you will receive.

Thus it is with faith and in hope that we look forward to the resurrection of the dead, and the life of the world to come.

Blessed be God Thrice Holy. Amen.

Appendix C

Faith and St. Thérèse

The experience of faith, doubt, almost to the point of despair, and triumph in the life of St. Thérèse of Lisieux is an interesting illustration of the challenge to faith and how it can be met. Three quotations from her autobiography are revealing.

The first is a comment describing her state in the spring of 1896, about the time she experienced the first unmistakable sign of the advanced stage of the disease that would bring about her death eighteen months later.

> At the time I was enjoying a faith that was so living and clear, that the thought of heaven filled me with happiness, and I was unable to believe there were really impious people who had no faith. I believed they were speaking against their own inner convictions when they denied the existence of heaven, that beautiful heaven where God

himself wanted to be their Eternal Reward.
During those very joyful days of the Easter
season, Jesus made me feel that there were
really souls who have no faith, and who,
through the abuse of grace, lose this precious treasure, the source of the only real
and pure joys. He allowed my soul to be
invaded by the thickest darkness, and the
thought of heaven, which up until then had
been so sweet to me, to be only a cause of
struggle and torment. This trial was to last
not a few days or a few weeks, it would end
only at the hour set by God himself and . . .
this hour has not yet come. I would like to
be able to put into words what I feel, but
alas! I believe this is impossible. One would
have to travel through this dark tunnel to
understand its darkness.[17]

The second testimony is taken from the same
part of her autobiography, in which the saint
describes her state of mind in June 1897, three
months before her death. Thérèse gives a vivid
description of the terrible dark doubt she was
experiencing and shows how a devout person can
be subject to temptations so severe that they
might seem to be of diabolical origin.

When I want to rest my heart, wearied by the darkness which surrounds it, by the memory of the luminous country to which I aspire, my torment redoubles; it seems to me that the darkness, borrowing the voice of sinners, says mockingly to me: "You are dreaming about the light, about a country fragrant with the sweetest perfumes; you are dreaming about the eternal possession of the Creator of all these things; you believe that one day you will walk out of this fog which surrounds you! Dream on, dream on; rejoice in death which will give you not what you hope for, but even deeper night, the night of nothingness."[18]

In the third selection St. Thérèse continues her account of the trial of faith, of which few, even those closest to her, were aware. She successfully concealed her sufferings until obedience forced her to reveal them to her superiors.

I may perhaps appear to you to be exaggerating my trial. In fact, if you go by the sentiments I express in my little poems composed this year, I must appear to you as a soul filled with consolations and one for whom the veil of faith is almost torn aside. It is no longer a veil for me, it is a wall which reaches right up to the heavens and hides the starry firmament. When I sing of the happiness of heaven, of the eternal possession of God, I feel no joy in this, for I sing simply what I WANT TO BELIEVE.[19]

————————

Those who suffer temptations against faith ought to be aware of St. Thérèse's experience. Cardinal Cahal Daly, former archbishop of Armagh and a well-known spiritual writer and philosopher, has said that among the many people in Europe who gave voice to the experience of nihilism, none was more eloquent than Thérèse of Lisieux precisely because she was a believer. Thérèse hung on to faith in the blackest darkness. Surely we can attribute this only to the gifts of the Holy Spirit, especially courage and wisdom. They are available to all Christians because of Baptism, and we should make use of them in every way, not only in times of trial but in everyday experience of life.

Appendix D

A Conversation With Joseph Cardinal Ratzinger, now Pope Benedict XVI

Shortly after I finished writing this book, Pope Benedict XVI was elected. He has written more than twenty books, several of which have been translated into English. He has participated in innumerable dialogues. I thought it would be interesting to give our readers an opportunity to share some of the new Pope's ideas on faith. They are drawn from *God and the World: Believing and Living in Our Time*, which grew out of conversations with a German journalist, Peter Seewald.

Readers are encouraged to go beyond the selections given here and study the whole of Cardinal Ratzinger's dialogue, in which many of the questions we have raised are examined more deeply and which reveals part of the fascinating personality of our new Pope.

SEEWALD: Many people are ready to accept the antichristian or antichurch stereotypes without further thought. The reason for this is often quite simply that we have lost hold of the signs and the content of the faith. We no longer know what they mean. Has the Church no more to say about this?

CARDINAL RATZINGER: There is no doubt that we live in a historical situation in which the temptation to do without God has become very great. Our culture of technology and welfare rests on the belief that basically we can do anything. Naturally, if we think like that, then life is restricted to what we can make and manufacture and demonstrate. The question about God leaves the stage.

If this attitude becomes generalized — and the temptation to do this is very great, because being on the lookout for God means in fact moving out onto another level of life, which seems in the past to have been more easily accessible — then the obvious thing is to say: What we have not made ourselves does not exist.

SEEWALD: There have been enough attempts, meanwhile, to construct an ethic without God.

CARDINAL RATZINGER: Certainly, and the calculus here is to find what is said to be most appropriate for man. On the other hand, we have attempts to manufacture man's inner fulfillment, his happiness, as a kind of product. Or, again, there are deviant, esoteric forms of religion on offer that seem to do without faith, that are often no more than techniques to achieve happiness.

All these ways of wanting the world to be measurable and to make do with one's own life are very closely related to the pattern of life and of existence in our time. The Word of the Church, on the other hand, seems to be coming from the past, whether because it is from long ago and no longer belongs to our time, or because it springs from a quite different kind of life that no longer seems to exist in our day. Certainly, the Church has not yet quite achieved the leap forward into the present day. The great task before us is so to fill with living experience the old, truly valid and great sayings that they become intelligible for people. We have a great deal to do there.[20]

SEEWALD: Is it not said that we should not make any image of God?

CARDINAL RATZINGER: This commandment has been transformed, insofar as God himself has given us his image. The Letter to the Ephesians [sic] says of Christ: "He is the image of God." And what is said about man in the creation story is fully realized in him.

Christ is the prototype of man. We cannot see in him the image of God in his eternal infinity, but we can see the image in which he chose to portray himself. From that point, we are no longer making an image, but God himself has shown us an image. Here he looks at us and speaks to us.

The image of Christ is of course not just a photo of God. In this picture of him who was crucified we see the whole life story of Jesus, above all the story of his inner life. That leads us into a way of seeing him in which our senses are opened up and then surpassed.

SEEWALD: How could one give an outline of Jesus in a few words?

CARDINAL RATZINGER: This always makes our words seem inadequate. Basically, Jesus is the Son of God, who comes from God and is at the same time true man. In him we meet not merely human genius and human heroism, but God, who becomes visible through him. One might say that in the body of Jesus, torn open on the Cross, we can see what God is like, that is, one who opens himself to us to this extent.[21]

SEEWALD: For many people, of course, it is not just incredible but presumptuous, a monstrous provocation, to believe that one single person, who was executed around the year 30 in Palestine, should be the Chosen and Anointed One of God, the "Christos", or Christ. That a single being should stand in the center of history.

In Asia there are hundreds of theologians who say that God is far too great and too inclusive to have incarnated himself in a single person. And is not faith in fact lessened thereby if the salvation of the whole world is supposed to be built upon one small point?

CARDINAL RATZINGER: This religious experience in Asia regards God as being so immeasurable, on one hand, and, on the other, our ability to conceive him as being so limited that in this view God is only able to represent himself to us in ever-changing aspects, in an unending myriad of reflections. Christ is then perhaps a more conspicuous symbol of God, but still just a reflection, which certainly does not comprehend the whole.

This is apparently an expression of the humility of man toward God. It is held to be quite impossible for God to enter into a single human being. And, thinking about it purely from the human point of view, we could perhaps expect nothing more than that we should only ever be able to see a little spark, a small section of God himself.

Yes. Being reasonable, one would have to say that God is far too great to enter into the littleness of a man. God is far too great for one idea or a single book to comprehend his whole word; only in many experiences, even contradictory experiences, can he give us reflections of himself. On the other hand, the humility would turn to pride if we were to deny God the freedom and the power and the love to make himself as small as that.

The Christian faith brings us exactly that consolation, that God is so great that he can become small. And that is actually for me the unexpected and previously inconceivable greatness of God, that he is able to bow down so low. That he himself really enters into a man, no longer merely disguises himself in him so that he can later put him aside and put on another garment, but that he becomes this man. It is just in this that we actually see the truly infinite nature of God, for this is more powerful, more inconceivable than anything else, and at the same time more saving.

If we took the other view, then we would necessarily have to live always with a mass of untruth. The contradictory fragments that are there in Buddhism, and likewise in Hinduism, suggest the solution of negative mysticism. But then God himself becomes a negation — and has in the end nothing positive or constructive to say to this world.

On the other hand, this very God, who has the power to realize Love in such a way that he himself is present in a man, that he is there and introduces himself to us, that he associates himself with us, is exactly what we need in order to escape from having to live to the end with fragments and half-truths.

That does not mean that we have nothing more to learn from other religions. Or that the canon of what is "Christian" is so firmly fixed that we cannot be led any farther. The adventure of Christian faith is ever new, and it is when we admit that God is capable of this that its immeasurable openness is unlocked for us.[22]

SEEWALD: In modern society people question whether there is such a thing as truth. That is turned against the Church, which still holds fast to this concept. You once said that the deep crisis of Christianity in Europe essentially originates in the crisis concerning its claim to truth. Why?

CARDINAL RATZINGER: Because no one any longer trusts himself to say that what faith asserts is true. People are afraid they might be acting intolerantly toward other religions or creeds. And Christians say among themselves that we have become afraid of the absolute quality of a claim to truth.

On one hand, that is in a way healthy. For if we lash out too readily, too casually with a claim to truth, or if we rest too comfortably upon it, we run the risk not only of becoming authoritarian, but also of elevating some secondary and temporary factor to the status of absolute truth.

A certain circumspection with regard to any claim to truth is entirely appropriate. But it ought not to lead us as far as dropping all claims to truth. That leaves us merely blundering about among various types of tradition.

SEEWALD: At any rate, boundaries are becoming genuinely less clear. Many people dream of a kind of casserole religion, with the most palatable ingredients carefully selected. People increasingly differentiate between "good" and "bad" religion.

CARDINAL RATZINGER: What is interesting is that the concept of tradition has to a great extent made redundant that of religion, and that of confession or denomination — and, thereby, that of truth. Particular religions are regarded as traditions. They are then valued as being "venerable", as "beautiful", and people say that whoever stands in one tradition should respect that one; another person, his own tradition; and everyone should respect each other's. At any rate, if traditions are all we have, then truth has been lost. And sooner or later we will ask what in fact traditions are for. And in that case a revolt against tradition is well founded.

I always recall the saying of Tertullian, that Christ never said "I am the custom", but "I am the truth". Christ does not just lend his weight to custom or tradition; on the contrary, he leads us right out of the customary way. He wants us to depart; he urges us to seek out what is true, whatever will bring us into the reality of the One who is the Creator and Redeemer of our own being. To that extent, we must regard circumspection as a serious obligation with respect to any claim to truth, but we must also have the courage not to lose hold of the truth, to stretch toward it and to accept it humbly and thankfully, whenever it is given to us.[23]

How You Can Help
the Franciscan Friars
of the Renewal

The day the Franciscan Friars of the Renewal left their original home in the Capuchin Order, we spoke at length with Mother Teresa. She told us to determine our apostolates carefully and to never change them. Following the example of the early Capuchins, we chose the physical care of the poor and evangelical preaching. Over the last twenty years we have tried to remain faithful to that vocation while seeking the other goal of our community, which is the reform of religious life and Catholic life in general. Along with many other people, we are convinced that Church reform is imperative at the present time and that it must begin with personal reform of the individual.

Since we have no visible means of support either for our own life or the work of the community, we depend completely on alms and support from generous friends. More than half of what we are given is distributed immediately to the poor, both in American cities like New York's Harlem and the Bronx, as well as in England and especially Honduras. Our own financial needs are minimal except for the cost of health and building insurance. Although we own no property, we are required by the Church to insure all the buildings we use. We are, of course, likewise required to have health insurance.

We would be grateful, if you feel inspired to do so, to receive some help from you. If you wish to help our community, make checks payable to Franciscan Friars of the Renewal; if you wish to help our work with the poor, we use our Padre Pio Shelter account as our general charities account. Any donations made to us will be used for a wide array of services, ranging from our hospital in Honduras to our shelter for the homeless. We will be happy to send you a little paper describing what we do.

Thanks be to God that we have received a good many vocations, and every year the numbers of both friars and sisters are growing. This also puts us under a considerable financial strain.

Any offerings can be sent to:

Fr. Benedict J. Groeschel, C.F.R.
Box 55
Larchmont, NY 10538

Notes

[1] Msgr. Ronald Knox's translation (New York: Sheed & Ward, 1956).

[2] See Fr. Benedict J. Groeschel, C.F.R., *From Scandal to Hope* (Huntington, Ind.: Our Sunday Visitor, 2002), 96–97.

[3] Matthias Scheeben, *The Mysteries of Christianity*, trans. Cyril Vollert, S.J. (St. Louis, Mo.: B. Herder, 1946), 3–4.

[4] John Henry Newman, *Idea of a University*, as quoted in *The Heart of Newman*, a synthesis arranged by Erich Przywara, S.J. (San Francisco: Ignatius Press, 1997), 124–125.

[5] John Henry Newman, "The Mysteriousness of Our Present Being," *Parochial and Plain Sermons* (IV) (San Francisco: Ignatius Press, 1997), 921.

[6] "Faith and Obedience," *Parochial and Plain Sermons* (III), op. cit., 535.

[7] Ibid., 535–536.

[8] Ibid., 537.

[9] See Luke Timothy Johnson's study, *The Real Jesus* (Harper San Francisco, 1997).

[10] "Mysteries in Religion" in *Parochial and Plain Sermons* (II).

[11] Archbishop Anthony Bloom, *Beginning to Pray* (New York: Paulist Press, 1970), 9–10. See also *The Journey Toward God*, 177–178.

[12] For an excellent popular review of the earliest Church Fathers see Rod Bennett, *Four Witnesses* (Ignatius Press, 2002).

[13] From "Contra Epistolam Manichæi quam vocant Fundamenti," in *Leaves from St. Augustine*, trans. Mary H. Allies, ed. T. W. Allies, K.C.S.G. (London: Burns and Oates, 1909), 302–303.

[14] The author used pseudonyms, or just initials, to refer to the principal players in this drama. Carrel is Louis Lerrac (his name spelled backward), Marie Bailly is Marie Ferrand, and M. is an intern.

[15] Alexis Carrel, *The Voyage to Lourdes*, trans. Virgilia Peterson (New York: Harper and Brothers, 1950; reprinted Real-View-Books, 1994), 75–77. See also Fr. Paul Glynn, *The Healing Fire of Christ* (Ignatius Press, 2003).

[16] Miguel de Unamuno, "The Atheist's Prayer," quoted in *The Journey Toward God*, compiled by Fr. Benedict J. Groeschel, C.F.R., and Kevin Perrotta (Ann Arbor, Mich.: Servant Publications, 2000), 168.

[17] From the autobiography of St. Thérèse of Lisieux, quoted in Guy Gaucher, *The Passion of Thérèse of Lisieux* (New York: Crossroad, 2001), 56–57.

[18] Ibid., 56.

[19] Ibid., 57.

[20] Joseph Cardinal Ratzinger, *God and the World: Believing and Living in Our Time*, trans. Henry Taylor (San Francisco: Ignatius Press, 2002), 27–28.

[21] Ibid., 24. (The citation referenced to the Letter to the Ephesians is actually from Colossians 1:15.)

[22] Ibid., 30–32.

[23] Ibid., 34–35.

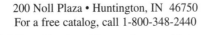